ZERO TIME
ZERO MISTAKE
ZERO COST

❧

A NEW WAY TO WORK

1st Edition

F.B. ENN

Note for Librarians: a cataloguing record for this
book that includes Dewey Classification and US
Library of Congress numbers is available from
the National Library of Canada. The complete
cataloguing record can be obtained from the
National Library's online database at:
www.nlc-bnc.ca/amicus/index-e.html
ISBN 1-4120-3293-8

Printed in Victoria, BC, Canada

TRAFFORD

This book was published *on-demand* **in
cooperation with Trafford Publishing.**
On-demand publishing is a unique process and
service of making a book available for retail sale
to the public taking advantage of on-demand
manufacturing and Internet marketing. **On-demand
publishing** includes promotions, retail sales,
manufacturing, order fulfilment, accounting and
collecting royalties on behalf of the author.

Suite 6E, 2333 Government St.,
Victoria, B.C. V8T 4P4, CANADA
Phone   250-383-6864
Toll-free   1-888-232-4444
Fax   250-383-6804
E-mail   sales@trafford.com
www.trafford.com/robots/04-1120.html

10   9   8   7   6   5   4   3   2   1

ABSTRACT

This book is about a problem solving principle which is designed to achieve zero time, zero mistake and zero cost in totality if practiced with a strong desire for the three zeros and the confidence that it will work sooner or later.

This principle is designed by integrating practical ideas to do things faster, better and cheaper such as "next definite step", "discontinue the work" and "what we want ultimately".

This principle is also flexible such that it allows readers to integrate this principle with readers' way of thinking in order to fulfill readers' wish with respect to time, quality and cost management.

F.B. Enn.
2004.

INTRODUCTION

Being able to solve a problem faster, better and cheaper has been the wish of many people.

Many books have been written with respect to either time management, quality control/assurance, cost control or the likes. However, if you apply those time management principle in isolation, you may compromise quality. Likewise, if you apply those cost control principle in isolation, you may compromise quality. Nevertheless, if you apply those quality control principle in isolation, you may compromise time and cost. In the end, many people just accept the so called balance between time, quality and cost.
Note : In this context, the term quality also include safety, health, environment (SHE) and reputation.

To the writer, achieving that perceived balance between these three important values to solve a problem is not good enough. You want to do things faster but nonetheless better and cheaper, don't you.

In this book, in order to fulfill that wish to achieve the three important values without compromising each other values, the writer will not talk about time, quality and cost in isolation, but in totality. The writer will also introduce the terms zero time, zero mistake, zero cost and a problem solving principle.

When a problem occur (or when your customer make an order) and you solve the problem (or deliver the required product/

service) immediately, you are deemed to do it at zero time. When the problem do not recur after you have solved the problem (or when your final product/service is accepted and no subsequent rejection is made), you are deemed to do it with zero mistake. When you solve the problem with no out-of-pocket money, you are deemed to do it with zero cost. Note: In this context, you are allowed to make mistake in your initial product in order to make zero mistake in your final product.

When you act before the problem occur (or when you deliver the product/service before the customer make the order), you are deemed to do it with negative time. When you solve the problem once and for all (or when you deliver a product/ service that exceed your customer's requirement), you are deemed to do it with negative mistake. When you make money, instead of incurring cost while you solve the problem, you are deemed to do it with negative cost.

That's impossible to be achieved. But that was also the remarks when somebody gave an idea of going to the moon. To achieve the three zeros, the writer believes in three things; a strong desire for the three negatives, a problem solving principle which is practicable but designed to achieve the three negatives and the confidence that it will work sooner or later. This is a new way to work.

We should target to achieve negative time, negative mistake and negative cost as in the real world, there are a lot of unforeseeable things that can obstruct our way. If we can't achieve the negatives, we may settle with the zeros. But if we target to achieve the zeros, then we may end up with the positives.

The problem solving principle which will be introduced by the writer is designed so that you will be close enough to achieve the three zeros, if not the three negatives by integrating the chosen formulas of getting the work done faster, better and cheaper.

Chapter 1: In The Space will explain the philosophies behind the problem solving principle uphold by this book.

Chapter 2: In The Air will illustrate the ingredients of this problem solving principle i.e. the formulas of getting the work done faster, better and cheaper which were derived from the philosophies explained in *Chapter 1*. The terms/formulas used in this book may not be having the same meaning as what you might have understood before reading this book. Well, it is the intended function that matter most, not what you call it.

Chapter 3: Down To Earth will explain how the formulas stated in *Chapter 2* were applied in piece meal basis to manage fast track projects by some reputable companies in the world.

Chapter 4: The Principle will illustrate how the formulas are integrated to form a simple but yet effective and efficient problem solving principle.

The ways on how this problem solving principle can be applied to solve simple to complicated problems are explained in *Chapter 5: Application*.

The Conclusion will summarize the contents of this book and anticipating the next edition in the near future.

If you have made up your mind before reading the whole book that its contents will not help you to achieve your desired zero time, zero mistake and zero cost, then the writer suggests that you take this book home, understand and integrate the contents with your way of thinking. Then you will see that your three zeros are not really that far away.

If you think that there will be nothing new to you in this book, look at it again, look at the definition of the terms used and if you are sure that it's nothing new, then you may take that this book is supporting and justifying your thinking/action in terms of time, quality and cost management.

Chapter 1 : In The Space

Problem, problem, problem.........This is what you face every time, every where. No matter what you do, no matter what science and technology do, no matter how smart you are, no matter how many problem solving books you have read, no matter how many consultants/advisors you have engaged, you can never escape from problem.

This book is not about telling you how to be free from problem but to show you some of the ways you can handle the problem, particularly in the interest of time, quality and cost.

First, let us look at the positive side of problem. Problem keep us wanting to improve ourselves, keep us wanting to adapt to our environment, keep us active, make us feel satisfied and good when we had solved it, make us matured, make us civilized; in other words it makes life going on and on. Imagine if there is no problem in this world; life will be so boring, everybody will stay as they are, no advancement in science and technology, policemen or you may be out of job, a lot of things will not exist, you will see only smiling faces, in other words life will be good as dead.

But we have to control or solve the negative side of the problem such that it will be to our advantage. There are many ways to solve a problem, depending on what you want and whichever way that suit you. However, in this book, the writer wants to show you how to solve the problem, having known the nature of the problem and your options such that you can solve it faster, better and cheaper; preferably close enough to achieve zero time, zero mistake and zero cost.

Problem can be due to its availability or unavailability to certain extent. Too much or too little can cause problem. Examples of problems due to their availability are uncontrolled fire, flood, typhoon, corrosion, erosion, vibration, uncontrolled use of drugs, nuclear weapons, etc. Examples of problems due to their unavailability are no money, no workers, no material/consumable, no tools/equipment, no procedure, no agreement, etc. All these problems can then lead to problems with respect to time, quality and cost.

Before we talk about problem solving principle or formulas, let us consider the following nature of problem and thus the problem solving philosophy:

Problem can never be eliminated. It can only be changed from one form to another form.

The writer believes at this point of time that not many readers agree to this philosophy. But whichever problems that you think you have eliminated, the writer is very sure that in reality none has been eliminated. The writer does not wish to discourage you about problem solving, but you have to face the reality and make your way through it. If God designed the problem to be eliminated, then there will be no more problem in this world and we will be good as dead.

When we had transport problem, we invented the car, airplanes and ship. But the transport problem was not eliminated. We have to maintain the car, airplanes and ship; we have to source for fuel, we have to set up a repair workshop, we have to deal with accidents and so on and so on. In this case, the transport problem in reality is transformed into maintenance problem and safety problem. So *problem cannot be eliminated but can be changed from one form to another form.*

When you had recurring quality problem in your company, you conducted the so called "root cause analysis". You found out that the root cause was incompetency of your staff. So you thought to eliminate the problem by conducting training to your staff. But the quality problem was not eliminated. You have to design and maintain the training system. You have to ensure that your staffs were not attending more training than working. In this case, the quality problem in reality is transformed into training's design problem and later training's maintenance problem. So here is another example where *problem cannot be eliminated but can be changed from one form to another form.*

When your car engine became hot, you found out that the water tank was empty, so you filled in water. In the next few days, the car engine became hot again and you filled in the water tank again. Then the car engine became hot again. Later you found out that the radiator was leaking. So you replaced the radiator and the car engine never became hot again. So you thought you had eliminated the problem. But the hot engine problem was not eliminated as you have new problem; you borrowed some money to buy the new radiator and the borrower is now chasing after you for payment. So here is another example where *problem cannot be eliminated but can be changed from one form to another form.*

Below are some examples of how we can handle problem but not eliminating it.

When we had too much or difficult work, we managed the work by delegating the work to others. But the "too much or difficult work" problem was not eliminated. We just transferred the problem to others. So *certain problem can be transferred to others*.

When you could not lift a heavy object, you used heavy lift tools/ equipment. But the lifting problem was not eliminated. You just transferred the problem to the tools/equipment which you need to maintain. So *certain problem can be transferred to an object*.

When we had a big task to build a big building, we divided the problem into various disciplines (civil, electrical, mechanical), various phases, use internal or external resources, we divided it into various importance (must do, should do or do nothing) and many other ways to divide the problem. So *certain problem can be divided into manageable parts*.

When someone told a politician that he has poverty problem in his area, the politician said that it was not a problem if compared to other political area which have more poverty problem. But the poverty problem was not eliminated. The politician just re-rated the problem. So *certain problem can be re-rated*.

When a country had poverty problem, the government did not use the money to subsidize the poor. Instead the government spent the money on development projects; building more industries which later would create job opportunities for the poor. So *certain problem can be solved by solving other problem*.

When a shopkeeper knew that there would be shortage of sugar in the market, he would keep a big stock of sugar and when the shortage occurred, he would raise the price of the sugar. The shopkeeper saw the opportunity to make more money when he saw the problem of the sugar's shortage coming in. So *certain problem can be turned into opportunities.*

When a critical machine was about to trip, an alarm would be flashed or sounded so that preventive action could be taken before it trip. *So a warning can be given before certain problem occur.*

When a tiger killed a cattle, they caught the tiger and put it in a cage. But the tiger problem was not eliminated. They just contained the tiger in the cage. So *certain problem due to its availability can be contained.*

When a construction worker worked in a construction site, he wore helmet to protect his head from falling object. But the falling object problem was not eliminated. He just shielded himself against the falling object. So *certain problem due to its availability can be shielded.*

When they saw a volcano, they ran away from it. But the volcano problem was not eliminated. They just kept themselves away from the volcano. So *certain problem due to its availability can be kept away.*

When a prey saw a predator, the prey would camouflage just like its surrounding. But the problem was not eliminated. So *certain problem due to its availability can be solved by camouflage.*

When a pipe engineer wanted to prevent corrosion of a pipe, he put a sacrificial anode. But the corrosion problem was not eliminated. He just sacrificed an anode to protect the pipe from corroding. So *certain problem due to its availability can be solved by sacrifice.*

When you saw your guest coming to your house, you quickly swept the rubbish under the carpet. But the rubbish problem was not eliminated. You just hid the rubbish problem. So *certain problem due to its availability can be hid.*

When you had no material, you created or acquired the material. But the problem is not eliminated as you need to create and maintain a system to create or acquire the material. So *certain problem due to its unavailability can be solved by creation or search and acquisition.*

When your fan was defective in your bedroom, you swapped with the portable fan in your living room. But the problem was not eliminated as you still need to repair the defective fan. So *certain problem due to its unavailability can be solved by swapping.*

When your car was not available as it broke down, you went to the office by bus. But the problem was not eliminated as you still need to repair the car. So *certain problem due to its unavailability can be solved by using other alternative.*

Now, lets see how the above problem solving philosophies may be applied, for example, to solve the problem of a tiger attacking your village.

Problem cannot be eliminated but can be changed from one form to another form
When you see the tiger, you may shoot the tiger to death. But you are not eliminating the problem. The problem of disturbing the food chain may arise; the animals that used to be the prey of the tiger may come back and destroy your crops.

Problem can be transferred to others
You may ask the zoo personnel to help you to catch the tiger.

Problem can be divided into manageable parts
You may divide the activity of hunting the tiger into the searching activity, the killing activity and the self-defense activity.

Problem can be transferred to an object
You may use a trap designed by the zoo personnel to catch the tiger.

Problem can be re-rated
You may tell the villagers that the tiger problem is common everywhere. In other places or previously there are more tigers than here/now.

Problem can be solved by solving other problem
You have a financial problem. So you may sell off all your cattle. The tiger may stop attacking your village as there are no more cattle .

Problem can be turned into opportunities
You may call in National Geographic or Discovery to your village and ask for some rewards for them to make a film out of your tiger hunting.

Warning can be given before certain problem occur
You may rear dogs so that the dogs will warn you by barking when the tiger approach your village.

Problem due to its availability can be contained
You may catch the tiger and put it in a cage.

Problem due to its availability can be kept away
You may ask the villagers to leave the village and stay away from the tiger.

Problem due to its availability can be hid
You may tell the villagers that there is no tiger and not to worry.

Problem due to its availability can be shielded
You may use a special shield on your neck and body to protect yourself against tiger claw or bite when you are hunting the tiger.

Problem due to its availability can be solved by sacrifice
You may sacrifice chicken before the tiger kill your cattle or people.

Problem due to its availability can be solved by camouflage
You may put a mask of a man at your back as tiger normally attack from your back and not from the front.

Problem due to its unavailability can be solved by creation or search and acquisition
Suppose that there is no trap to catch the tiger. You may make (create) the trap or search and borrow (acquire) one from the zoo.

Problem due to its unavailability can be solved by swapping
Suppose that one of your trap in frequently visited area by the tiger is defective. You may swap the trap with the one used in other area which are not frequently visited by the tiger.

Problem due to its unavailability can be solved by using other alternative
Suppose that you do not have a shotgun to shoot the tiger. You may use bow and arrow as an alternative.

The above examples are just some of the problem solving philosophies that you may use to solve problem, but you can never eliminate the problem. To put the above problem solving philosophies into practice, you need to consider and handle potential problems as problem will change from one form to another form.

This book is about how we can use and turn the above problem solving philosophies into workable formulas as shown in Chapter 2 and integrate those formulas in Chapter 4 such that it will help us to be close enough to achieve zero time, zero mistake and zero cost in totality.

Chapter 2: In The Air

Why zero time, zero mistake and zero cost? In the near future it will not be something nice to know, but a must know thing. Today some quality gurus are preaching about zero rework (mistake) and some safety practitioners are implementing zero incident program. Fast forwarding managers are talking about wanting things to be done by today if not yesterday. Some businessmen are already talking about zero cost. Soon these drives for the zeros will become normal and those who are ignorant will soon lose out in any field where they compete with others. Therefore, before the time come, let us be ahead of the game by talking about the three zeros and the problem solving principle to achieve the three zeros in totality, not in isolation.

The problem solving principle, which will be explained in Chapter 4 are made of the formulas to get the work done faster, better and cheaper. These formulas are not rocket science; they are simple, common sense and may have been used consciously or unconsciously in your day-to-day work. The following formulas are derived from the problem solving philosophies explained in Chapter 1.

Work can be done <u>faster</u> by the following:
- Next definite step;
- Taking opportunity;
- What we have/can;
- Criticality;
- Selected part;
- Taking certain precautions;

- Asking the specialist;
- Root cause;
- Simultaneous;
- Prepared/local resources;
- Swapping;
- Special tool ;
- Target to complete earlier;
- Partial delivery;
- Original supplier.

Work can be done <u>better</u> by the following:
- Next definite step;
- Selected part;
- Taking certain precautions;
- Remaining part of the problem;
- What we want ultimately;
- Asking the specialist;
- Root cause;
- Life cycle cost;
- Special tool;
- Partial delivery;
- Conditions of acceptance;
- Original supplier.

Work can be done <u>cheaper</u> by the following:
- Next definite step;
- Taking opportunity;
- What we have/can;
- Criticality;
- Selected part;
- Taking certain precautions;
- Asking the specialist;
- Root cause;
- Owned/local resources;

- Partial delivery;
- Cost/reward sharing;
- Life cycle cost;
- Original supplier;
- Middling.

The terms/formulas used in this book may not be having the same meaning as what you might have understood before reading this book. It is the intended function that matter most, not what you call it. Therefore, please read carefully and understand the meaning to get the most out of this book.

Next Definite Step

When we face a problem, we tend to "react" to the problem. When there is a fire, we tend to fight the fire. When our boss want us to do "A", we will do "A" exactly as told. When we are hungry, naturally we tend to eat.

"Reacting" is the key to survival. But "reacting" also keep us one step behind the problem. If we do not react promptly for critical problem, it may have caused intolerable damage before we can control it.

Imagine if you can go back to the past. You may be able to prevent the mistake that you are making now; you may be able to stop doing the work that caused the fire now. Likewise, if you can go to the future and come back to the present time, you may be able to know what should be done in the present time; you may be able to know that fighting the fire the way you are doing now will or will not work. Going to the future, in this context, is to prepare the **next definite step**.

A **next definite step** is a future step which is definite to be done regardless of the preceding step and which will be rewarded or recognized. This formula is derived from the philosophy *problem can be solved by solving other problem.* By doing the **next definite step** before the preceding step(s), you will be;

- Able to know the actual things to be done in the preceding step(s), thus reduce unnecessary work and promote zero mistake;
- Able to do the preceding step(s) without additional cost by using the resources of the **next definite step** and/or the reward of the **next definite step,** thus achieving zero cost;
- Ahead of time to get the reward/recognition and therefore deemed to have achieved negative time.

In a conventional way of working, you will do things in sequence, i.e. Step A, followed by Step B, then Step C, Step D, Step E and so on and so on. In a new way to work, you may start with Step E, then maybe Step C, then Step E again, then maybe Step A in a zigzag manner. Step E, where you start, is the **next definite step.**

In order to do the **next definite step** before the preceding step(s), you may carry out the preparatory work of the **next definite step** or doing part of the **next definite step** up to the point where the preceding step(s) is still not required to be done. While you **prepare the next definite step**, you **take the opportunity** to do the preceding step(s).

The **next definite step** is a kind of forward thinking. You go on to proceed with your future major plan despite the problem that you are facing now and you **take the opportunity** of preparing the **next definite step** to solve the problem that you are facing now.

The **next definite step** can be either one or the combination of the following, whichever is practical and effective to you at that point of time:

- Preparing or doing part of the future step which will be rewarded/ recognized and which do not require the preceding step(s) to be done in order to know what is actually required to be done in the preceding step(s);
- Going to the work site to see the opportunities apart from the constraints/obstacles;
- Asking for clarifications that will make the work easier; asking the cause of the problem and alternative solutions, asking the risk/ **criticality** of doing nothing, asking where is it critical, asking what had been done to solve the problem, the lessons learnt and the recommendations, asking who can help you, what tools to be used and asking for more details.

<u>Example 1</u>

You want to renovate your house. In a conventional manner, you would do the following:

Step 1: You imagine what will be the best way to renovate your house or buy some magazines about house renovation;

Step 2: You ask the contractor to renovate your house the way you want;

Step 3: Contractor will procure the material to renovate your house.

In this manner, you may most probably end up making requirement which is unrealistic, out of your budget or take too long to complete. In a new way to work, you may do part of Step 3 first i.e. you ask the Contractor of the available material for your renovation work, then you go to Step 2 to ask the contractor what are the alternatives that you have to renovate your house with the available material and then you go to Step

1 i.e. to select the one alternative with some minor modification to meet your requirement with respect to schedule, quality and budget.

Example 2

You want to go to for a jungle tracking with your family. You want to know what need to be prepared/brought for the jungle tracking. You ask your friends but none have gone to the jungle tracking route that you are going to take. Your friends have experience with other jungle tracking route and they advise you to bring some items. You also think what to bring. Then you bring along those advised/thought items which may later turn out to be not relevant or too heavy for you and your family to bring. In a new way to work, you may go to the actual site to experience the small part of the jungle tracking yourself to find out what you actually need to bring after considering the available facilities and the obstacles/ constraint before you do the actual wholesome jungle tracking with your family.

Example 3

You have been assigned by your boss to prepare a presentation material which will be presented to a management committee to cover your department's future plans. In the conventional way, you would;
Step 1 : Prepare the material;
Step 2: Get your boss to review the material;
Step 3. Make correction;
Step 4 : Present to the committee.

In this case, instead of straight-away preparing the material, one of the **next definite step** is Step 4, so first you may prepare to do Step 4 by talking to one of the Committee members and ask his expectation of the presentation material. You may also ask what had been done in the past to make such presentation, what was the lessons learnt and improvement to be made in this presentation, which part of the presentation is critical to the committee, why such presentation is required and what are your alternatives. By doing so, you are ahead of time (at least you are aware of the questions to be posed by the Committee member) and be able to identify the actual required material or alternative material to be prepared.

Another possibility of the **next definite step** is Step 2, so first you prepare to do Step 2 by talking to your boss on the structure/format of the presentation material before preparing your material. This will save your time from doing unnecessary work. The choice of which **next definite step** to be taken first depend on the practicality. Ideally you should go first to the major step (in this case Step 4), and from there you will start the preceding step(s).

The potential problem of preparing the **next definite step** is that you may not have the resources or opportunity to start the work. So you may do the preceding step(s) first using **what we have/can** but **taking the opportunity** to do the **next definite step** whenever possible.

Take the Opportunity

We tend to see more problems than opportunities. We also tend to consider one problem at a time. Have you ever had this experience; when you returned home, your wife asked you to buy something; when you returned home after buying the thing, your wife asked you to fetch your children; when you returned home after fetching your children, your wife asked you to pay the electric bills.

Imagine if you can turn the problems into opportunities and consider many problems at a time. You would had bought the thing and took the opportunity to fetch your children and paid the electric bill before you returned home. Therefore, though you may solve the problem physically one at a time, but first you should consider many problems at a time.

Taking the opportunity here refers to either one or the combination of the following, whichever is practical and effective to you at that point of time;

- Doing the work without additional cost with the resources assigned to other work at same/nearby area. You hire a grass cutter to cut the grass at your house compound. You may ask the grass cutter to pick up any rubbish found without additional charge while he cut the grass;.
- **Taking the opportunity** to get partial payment after making **partial delivery.** You are supposed to deliver three pair of shoes to your customer. You may deliver one pair first and ask for a 30% partial payment from your customer;
- Selling the problem;
  - ✓ To offer the problem to those who need the problem. A tall grass at your house compound may be sold to those who rear cattle;
  - ✓ To advertise something while solving the problem. There is a safety crisis in your plant. In resolving the crisis, your staff wear a branded safety shoes. You ask the shoes maker to sponsor the exercise as your staff will advertise the use of the safety shoes in TV.
- To reuse the problem against the origin of the problem. A missile directed to you may be redirected to those who launched it.

This formula is derived from the philosophy *problem can be turned into opportunities.*

By **taking the opportunity**, you may achieve zero cost or even make money and therefore deemed to achieve negative cost.

Taking the opportunity may answer the question, "Who should do the work"? This question is always a big debate in big companies. As the company grow bigger, the tendency to specialize increase and the employee is hired to do what he is specialized in. A plant operator, upon seeing a bulb blown off will instead of changing it himself, will record the defect in his diary, then he transfer it in a computer, then he send the electronic message to company's electrician to fix the defect, then he call for a meeting to follow up on the implementation, then when nothing is done, he call in a contractor to do it. Despite that the plant operator is in position, is capable and has the opportunity to replace the blown bulb quickly, he tend to leave it to the electrician because it is not his job. Imagine the wastage of time and money by this organization setup. **Take the opportunity** here means the ideal person to change the bulb is the plant operator himself because he is in position and knowledgeable to do the work and it will not take more time than his core work i.e. to operate the plant.

The potential problem with **taking the opportunity** is that you may end up doing more opportunity works than doing your core work. So you may **take the opportunity** to solve the problem temporarily only using **what we have/can**.

What We Have/Can

We tend to call in the mechanic first when we cannot start our car. We tend to seek psychiatrist help first when we had a personal problem. We tend to call in the quality guru first when we had quality problem in our company.

You call in the mechanics only to find out later that your wife had called in your neighbor who is good at car engine. You call in the psychiatrist only to find out later that your wife had called in the same psychiatrist who could not solve the problem. You call in the quality guru only to find out later that the noncompliance of the existing quality system was the cause of the quality problem. The moral of the story is before you jump to a decision, "ask what had been done to solve the problem", "start where you have stopped" and "do not reinvent the wheel". Furthermore, it take time to seek external help as he has to mobilize and to understand the problem while the problem had caused the damage before he come for the rescue.

Note : There are times where seeking external help is required; see **ask the specialist** in later pages of this book.

If nothing had been done to solve the problem, then you may first try to solve it by yourself or by your in-house manpower. You may see yourself whether the car battery is working (by switching on the lamp) or whether there is fuel in your car before you call in the mechanic. You may ask your close friends/relatives to give you free advise before you call in the psychiatrist. You may check whether your internal quality system is being complied before you call in the quality guru to re-engineer your quality system.

You may have had this experience; you went to a brainstorming session to solve some issues in your company. Then your team came out with an action list and closed out the brainstorming session. But the issue was not resolved. Another team was formed to brainstorm and to come out with a solution. A long list of action item was generated, which in principle was an old wine in the new bottle. The brainstorming session continued in the next cycle but the issue was never resolved. Why? It is partly because we always start from the beginning again, not from where we stopped. We came out with a solution but we never implement the solution or follow up on its implementation. We hardly ask "what had been done previously to resolve the issue, was it done, is it working"? Instead, we start with the brainstorming again hoping to find a new solution.

Asking what had been done or what do we have or what can we do to solve the problem in this context are called **what we have/can**. It also covers things like use of one than rather multiple, fixing the schedule than rather on as-and-when required basis, use **prepared/local/owned resources- special tool, swapping** , doing easy-to-do things or anything practical.

What had been done <u>elsewhere</u> to solve similar problem? Do we have or can we do that?

Asking **what we have/can** may generate alternative solutions and you may select the one which is practicable to solve the problem faster and cheaper.

The problem of using **what we have/can** is that it may not be good enough to solve the problem. So you may start at **selected part.**

Criticality

Let's consider **criticality** before we consider **selected part**.

Should I do nothing or do something about a problem? Where/when is the problem critical? What is the risk **(criticality)** of doing nothing?

You may classify the criticality of the problem into three level, i.e. critical, non-critical or negligible. You may also classify them into five (5) level, i.e. very critical, critical, semi-critical, non-critical and negligible. The number of these levels should be the same as the number of the available solutions to the problem. If you have three (3) level of criticality, then your solution may also be three (3) level, i.e. do nothing for negligible problem, do something small for non-critical problem or do something big for critical problem. If you have five (5) level of criticality, then your solution may also be five (5) level i.e. do nothing, do something quite small, do something small, do something big, do something very big. So you may apply the solutions at appropriate level of criticality.

One of the way to determine the criticality of the problem is by asking the following questions:
• Consequence: What is the consequence of doing nothing with respect to SHE, economic and reputation?
• Probability: What is the probability that the (adverse) consequence will be likely to happen or when is the problem will be likely to happen or how often did the problem occur?

The **criticality** (or called risk) is the consequence multiply by the probability. Both the consequence and the probability may be classified into three (3) level i.e. High (H), medium (M) or low (L). So the criticality (consequence x probability) can be classified as negligible (L x L), non-critical (M x L, H x L,) and critical (H x H, H x M).

The criticality of a problem can be determined by the sample Criticality Assessment Matrix as per the table in the next page. This sample is not meant to be universal. You may design your own Criticality Assessment Matrix that suit your environment.

Criticality Assessment Matrix

	CONSEQUENCE of Doing Nothing			PROBABILITY of the Consequence of Doing Nothing		
L e v e l	Safety, Health & Environment (SHE)	Economic	Reputation	Never heard or less likely to occur	Had occurred elsewhere or likely to occur	Had occurred locally or more likely to occur
1	No injury. Slight environmental effect but within statutory limit	Cost of doing nothing < cost of making good	Local public awareness	NEGLIGIBLE (C1)	NON-CRITICAL (C2)	NON-CRITICAL (C3)
2	Minor First Aid or Medical Treatment Case Exceed statutory limit for < 1 day	Cost of doing nothing > cost of making good	Concern from local /regional public or political attention	NON-CRITICAL (C4)	NON-CRITICAL (C5)	CRITICAL (C6)
3	Lost Time Incident or Permanent Disability or Fatality or Fire Exceed statutory limit for > 1 day	Cost of doing nothing > 5 times cost of making good or higher by 10,000 dollars, whichever is higher	Negative image in local or foreign media	NON-CRITICAL (C7)	CRITICAL (C8)	CRITICAL (C9)

Example 1

- Describe the problem.
  - ✓ The general service water pipeline is corroding.

- Determine the consequence of doing nothing.
  - ✓ Pipe leak may occur . No impact on SHE and reputation. The cost of making good the pipe is 100 dollar. Cost of doing nothing is 50 dollar. Therefore the **cost of doing nothing < cost of making good** (refer column **Economic Level 1**).

- Determine the Probability of the consequence of doing nothing.
  - ✓ The probability of pipe leak is more likely as it **had occurred locally** (refer column **had occurred locally**).

- Determine the Criticality of doing nothing.
  - ✓ The criticality of doing nothing is non-critical (see box C3) , therefore do something small about it such as painting the pipeline.

<u>Example 2</u>

- Describe the problem.
  - ✓ The mesh of the bicycle's basket is too big to bring the tool.

- Determine the Consequence of doing nothing.
  - ✓ No impact on economic or reputation. The hand tool to be brought in the basket may drop, stuck at the bicycle's wheel, cause sudden stoppage of the bicycle and injured (**minor first aid** - refer column **SHE Level 2**) the cyclist.

- Determine the Probability of the consequence of doing nothing.
  - ✓ The probability of the cyclist having minor first aid for falling from bicycle caused by the basket is likely as it had occurred elsewhere (refer column **had occurred elsewhere**).

- Determine the Criticality of doing nothing.
  - ✓ The criticality of doing nothing is non-critical (see box C3) , therefore do something small about it such as wrapping a plastic in the basket to cover the big mesh.

Example 3

- Describe the problem.
  - ✓ To decide whether to ask the car driver/passenger to put on the safety belt while driving in the gazette plant.

- Determine the Consequence of doing nothing.
  - ✓ No impact on economic (no police fine as this is a gazette area) or SHE. The reputation of the plant as the safe plant to work can be affected as it can create **negative image in local or foreign media** - refer column **Reputation Level 3**.

- Determine the Probability of the consequence of doing nothing.
  - ✓ The probability of getting such reputation is likely as it had occurred elsewhere (refer column **had occurred elsewhere**).

- Determine the Criticality of doing nothing.
  - ✓ The criticality of doing nothing is critical (see box C8), therefore do something big about it such as penalize those who do not put on safety belt.

You may classify the consequence or the probability into five (5) level i.e. very high, high, medium, low and very low. So you may also end up into five (5) level of criticality.

By knowing the criticality of the problem, you will be able to apply the appropriate solution, set priorities and therefore optimize the use of your time and resources. In other words, you can do things faster, better and cheaper with the sense of criticality. You may put your utmost attention on critical part, you give some attention to non-critical part and you may do nothing at negligible part. You may also do nothing where doing something can cause more harm than good.

Having known the criticality, the next step is to know **selected part**.

Selected Part

We tend to apply a solution to the whole problem. When we have a corroded pipeline, we tend to replace the whole pipeline. When our staff is not performing, we tend to fire him straight-away. When we have used our clothing, we tend to wash them straight-away.

A solution can never be applicable to all problems. Welding is only applicable to metals while bra is only applicable to woman, at least at the time of writing this book.

A solution may also be applied to either a critical part, non critical part or negligible part, depending on the level of your solutions (see **criticality**).

Application of a solution also depend on your confidence of the success of the solution. You would apply a solution, starting from a critical part if your level of confidence on the success of the solution is high. On the other hand, you would apply a solution, starting from non-critical part or changeable part if your level of confidence on the success of the solution is low because if anything go wrong, then the impact would be low or you can change place. When the solution is proven working, then you will shift it to the critical part of the problem.

Application of a solution also depend on its practicality. You would apply a practicable solution first as a temporary solution, then you apply the difficult-to-do but effective solution later when you have the required resources and opportunity.

So you apply a solution at **selected part** i.e. first or later (depending on the availability of resources and opportunity), starting from critical or non-critical/changeable part (depending on your confidence) at the applicable part. You do welding first (if you have the resources and opportunity), starting from the critical part of the pipe (if your confidence on the success of welding is high) at the metallic part. This formula is derived from the philosophy *problem can be divided into manageable parts*.

So you may do things better, faster and cheaper with the sense of **selected part**. However, the problem of focussing on the **selected part** is that your work may not be adequate to solve the problem. To mitigate this problem, you **take certain precautions**.

Taking Certain Precautions

When we have found a solution, we tend to think that's all for now. When we have decided to do something, we tend to forget the potential problem. In short, there is no perfect solution that will be free from potential problem.

Taking certain precaution is about anticipating potential time, quality and cost problem when you want to do something and preparing to mitigate that potential problem. This formula is derived from the philosophy *problem cannot be eliminated*. There will certainly be new problem coming out when a problem had been solved.

Taking certain precaution can be either one or the combination of the following, whichever is practical and effective to you at that point of time:

For potential quality problem
- Modifying or increasing/decreasing **what we have/can** to *contain, keep away, shield, hide, camouflage, sacrifice, create, swap, use other alternative, re-rate* the potential problem;
  - ✓ You are required to sing a song to entertain your retiring colleague. But you cannot sing (*problem due to its unavailability*). You can only make a speech (**what we have/can**). The potential problem is that it may be boring if you make a speech. So you make the speech with jokes (modifying **what we have/can** as an *alternative*) to entertain your retiring colleague;
  - ✓ Its going to be cold (*problem due to its availability*). You have no sweater. You have only T-shirts (**what we have/can**). So you mitigate the potential problem (cold) by wearing lots of T-shirts (increasing **what we have/can** to *shield against the problem*);
- Using **special tool** for difficult work process;
- Audit/check on its compliance to what was planned.

For potential time problem
- Negotiate (see **asking specialist**) with supplier;
- **Learn and teach others to do** the work;
- Using **special tool** for low productivity work process.

For potential cost problem
- Negotiate (see **asking specialist**) with supplier;
- **Learn and teach others to do** the work;
- Use **original suppliers**.

For potential time/quality/cost problem

- Supply to your supplier with your **special tool** to improve the delivery period or work quality but charge your supplier the rental rate;
- Seeking lessons learnt and recommendations from past practitioners;
- Create a system to warn you of the upcoming failure, make what you do changeable and accessible promptly in case of anything go wrong;
- Making **partial delivery** to your customer for his **conditions of acceptance** and partial payment;
- Do nothing where the risk of doing nothing is negligible or doing something can cause more harm than good.

The problem with **taking certain precautions** is that it may not be good enough to solve the problem. So you may find the **root cause.**

Root Cause

What is the problem? Why (the problem)?

You want to know the cause of the problem so that you can solve the problem. When your car engine become hot, you find out that the water tank is empty so you fill in water. In the next few days, the car engine become hot again and you fill in the water tank again. The empty water tank is the immediate cause and by addressing the immediate cause, you will only solve the problem temporarily because the problem will recur. You need to find out the **root cause** in order to solve the problem permanently. But it does not mean that you have to forget about addressing the immediate cause because if you do not fill in water your car engine will remain hot. You need to address both the immediate cause (to fix the problem) and the **root cause** (to solve the problem permanently).

Addressing the **root cause** of a problem will prevent recurrence of the problem. The **root cause** can be determined by asking the question why, why, why and why again to such level that you considered that you had found the root cause. In reality, this level is subjective; when you have a fever, the immediate cause can be due to infection. So you take aspirin but the fever come back. A doctor may diagnose and may find out that your antibody is not capable to fight the infection and may conclude that the cause is HIV. Therefore the **root cause** is that you may had performed homosexual activity. So the permanent solution is to use condom. However, a religious person may conclude that the **root cause** is because you had committed the sin, so the permanent solution is not to commit the sin. A lawyer may think that the **root cause** is the ineffectiveness of the existing law and order to handle homosexual activity, so the permanent solution is to change the law. The political opposition party would think that the **root cause** is the ineffectiveness of the ruling party to combat homosexual activity, so the permanent solution is to change the ruling party.

The **root cause** of a problem can be due to the problem of design, construction, operation and/or maintenance. The **root cause** can also be due to the problem of the procedure, people (competency, attitude, communication), material, tools/equipment and/or money. Looking for the **root cause** depend on what you are prepared to change to prevent the problem from recurring.

To the writer, after you had found the so called **root cause**, you ask, "What is the work that we do (not the work that we don't do) that caused the **root cause**? Why do we need to do that work? Can that work be substituted by other ongoing work"?

These are strategic questions because the solution to "the work that we do" will definitely be within our control and will be very easy to do (zero cost and zero time) i.e. **discontinue the work that caused the problem where the work can be substituted by other ongoing work**. By discontinuing the work, you may also achieve negative cost as you may save cost by doing so. This is a new way to work. This formula is derived from the philosophy *problem cannot be eliminated; so don't create problem*. So try first <u>not</u> to do something and create problem to solve a problem.

For example, you think that lack of quality work in your workplace is due to incompetency of your staff. Normally, you will conduct training to address this root cause. Then you will face another problem i.e. to find out the methodology, resources, time and money to train your staff. But if you find out first what is the work that you do (than rather the work that you don't do) that caused incompetency of your staff, you may find out that either you conduct job rotation too soon that your staff cannot specialize on one job or you give them a lot of non-core work that make your staff no time to learn on their core job or you hire a general worker to do specialist work or your give confusing/unclear requirements that none of your staff can comply. So try first to discontinue those works (if you can substitute with other ongoing work) before you jump to train your staff.

That's why (the writer guessed) most religion tell us a lot more about "don't do this and this" than rather "do this and this" because "don't do" is the easier way to prevent all sort of problems in this world. Furthermore, if you start to think about "what is the thing that we don't do that caused the problem", then you will start to create a system to do the thing that you think should be done. Then you will create another problem, i.e. to maintain the system that you had created. Then you have to create another system to maintain your maintenance system. In the end, you have created a lot of problems by just creating one work. That's why problems can never end in this world. It is just like energy; you cannot destroy it; it just change from one form to another.

You may determine the **root cause** by asking the following questions:

- What are the possible causes? Can we confirm the possible causes quickly? If yes, proceed to confirm, if no, then ask the following questions;
- Where could the problem be, but is not happening? What is the difference in that area from the problem area? Is any of the possible causes unique to the problem area?
- When was the first time the same problem was observed? What is the changes just before the first time the same problem was observed? Can the any of the possible causes be related to that changes? Is the timing of the failure predictable (is it age-related)? Is there any symptom before it fail?
- What is the arrangement to prevent the problem. Is any of the possible causes deviating from that arrangement?

The common answer (possible cause) to the questions above will be the most likely cause. You may then confirm the cause by testing/simulation and monitor for any recurrence of the problem. Then you may find out what is the root cause (the work that we do that caused the cause of the problem) and discontinue the work where the work can be substituted by other ongoing work.

If the above questions could not lead you to the **root cause**, then you may ask;

- What was the possible causes that was ruled out? Is the assumption still valid?

- Is the problem genuine? Is the measurement right?
- Are the given information correct?

Example of finding the **root cause** of your car engine becoming hot:

- What are the possible causes? *You don't know at all because you know nothing about car engine;*
- Where could the problem be but is not happening? *My neighbor had the same car brand and model but he does not seem to have the problem.* What is the difference in your neighbor's car and your car? *You also don't know because everything look the same;*
- When was the first time the car engine became hot? *Last week.* What is the changes just before the first time the car engine became hot? *I had a car accident and they changed my <u>radiator</u>, absorber and head lamp. So these are the possible causes.* Is the timing of the failure predictable? *No.* Is there any symptom before it fail? *Yes, my temperature indicator rise up;*
- What is the arrangement to prevent the car engine become hot? *So you ask around and you find out that the arrangement to prevent your car engine become hot are no leaking water tank, no leaking <u>radiator</u> or no defective water pump.* Is any of the possible causes (<u>radiator</u>, absorber and head lamp) deviating from that arrangement? *Yes, could be the radiator that you had changed is leaking.*

The common possible cause from the questions above is the radiator. Then you confirm the cause (radiator) by testing at the workshop. Later, you find out it's confirmed leaking. So you ask, "What do I do that caused the cause (leaking radiator) of the problem?" You find out that;

- You changed the radiator because your radiator was knocked down during an accident;
- You changed the radiator at XYZ's Workshop;

- You knocked somebody's car because you drink a lot and got drunk.

Obviously you cannot discontinue changing the radiator because you need to change your original radiator which was knocked down. But you may solve this problem permanently by;
- discontinuing going to XYZ's Workshop in the future because you had other choices of workshop that can give good car repair service;
- discontinuing getting drunk if you can substitute drinking with other ongoing hobbies.

The potential problem of finding the **root cause** is that the **root cause** may not be found, difficult to be addressed or may not be relevant in solving the problem. So <u>if the problem is predictable</u>, based on time (age related) or condition, then you may take proactive action by applying the temporary solution or do **what you want ultimately** for **remaining part of the problem** before the problem recur. In this way, you can still prevent the problem from recurring but you need a continuous effort to act just before the problem recur. However, <u>if the problem is critical</u>, and though the root cause can be found and be addressed, you may also want to do **what you want ultimately** before the problem recur in order to assure zero mistake.

Remaining Part of the Problem

When we had solved a problem temporarily, we tend to forget to solve the **remaining part of the problem**. The **remaining part of the problem** can be the other difficult-to-do part of the problem or other potential area that can be affected by similar problem or the back-up/contingency plan. This formula is derived form the philosophy *problem can be divided into manageable parts*.

The **remaining part of the problem** can also be the action to be taken before the same problem recur at the same area. This is a proactive step where you take action before something fail. Something can be predicted to fail based on history. Something fail at fixed schedule (time based) while some other thing will fail based on some symptoms (condition based). While others fail randomly.

Depend on the criticality of the failure, you may let it run to failure or you take proactive action before it fail. For critical failure which is time based or condition based, you may arrange to take proactive action at an opportunity just before the predicted failure. For critical failure which is random, you may put a standby unit.

By considering the **remaining part of the problem**, it will lead you to take action before the problem recur and hence you are deemed to achieve **negative time** for future problem.

What We Want Ultimately

We tend to be contented with what we have achieved. We tend to accept things the way it is. Successful man always want to improve his life continuously. This so called "greed" - never happy with what we have - that made human being to progress and become what they are now.

What do you want to do? Depending on the criticality of the problem, you may want to do something small or something very big.

For critical problem, you may want to do something very big and make a high target. If you want a monthly salary of 1,000 dollars, you will hardly get 2,000 dollars but instead you may get 900 dollars. In reality, there will be a lot of uncontrollable circumstances, so you may get something smaller from what you want, even with good planning. That's why you should target negative time/mistake/cost to get the three zeros.

A **what we want ultimately** is a product/service that will not only meet your customer's requirement but exceed your customer's requirement. Therefore it will help you to achieve negative mistake.

Who is your customer? If you work for your employer, then your employer is your customer. If you built a house for your family, then your family is your customer. If you want to buy a shirt for yourself, then you yourself is the customer. If you make a decision, then whoever that will be affected by your decision is your customer. And never forget God as your customer in everything you do.

What is the product/service that exceed your customer requirement? If your customer want a 20" TV, do not assume that if you give him a 24" TV, then you will exceed his requirement. The 24" TV may not fit in the cabinet of your customer and therefore do not meet his requirement. You have to ask your customer what is the thing that exceed his requirement.

Sometime you cannot ask the customer what is the thing that exceed his requirement. You have to make some assumptions. To the writer, a **what we want ultimately**, subject to your customer's correction/ confirmation, is the thing that solve your customer's problem once & for all i.e.;

- It meet the customer requirement but yet;
- So flexible that it can solve the customer's other problems such that;

- It boost the customer's profit or the product is having low **life cycle cost;**
- Make the customer feel very safe and secured and;
- Boost the customer reputation or the product/service is recognized worldwide as the best product/service.

Note : This definition may not fit for customer such as God.

Is the PETRONAS Twin Tower a **what we want ultimately?** Most probably yes.

The PETRONAS Twin Tower is built once and for all; to meet the basic requirement as the PETRONAS central building but yet flexible that it is also the public shopping complex and recreational area. It was built such that it has boost PETRONAS reputation as the giant oil/gas/petrochemical company, probably very safe to stay in with the safety/security features of the building and recognized to be the tallest twin building in the world when this book was written. The **life cycle cost** is probably low due to use of stainless steel material which hardly corrode over time. Imagine the space saving in the expensive land compare to building a lower central building that occupy more expensive land area. And finally, imagine the revenue and profit to the country with the incoming tourists.

While preparing to get **what you want ultimately** for a problem, you may take the opportunity to prepare the **next definite step** of another problem.

The problem of getting **what you want ultimately** is that it may be difficult for you to get it. So you may find a specialist to do it for you and you **ask the specialist** to get a good deal.

Ask the Specialist (Supplier)

We tend to do everything by ourselves. We tend to waste our time trying to do specialized work or labor intensive work (but non-value added to our skill or knowledge) ourselves only to find later that it will be more cost effective, faster and better if we out source the work to supplier (or specialist).

You may ask the supplier bluntly to do the work for you free of charge (FOC) by either one or the combination of the following, whichever is practical and effective to you at that point of time:
- You will increase the supplier's business volume by recommending the product/service to other clients;
- To prove that it will work for the supplier to market its product to other clients;
- **Cost/reward sharing**.

If the above does not work, then consider **asking the specialist** by making an inquiry and negotiation to get a good deal. This formula is derived from the philosophy *problem can be transferred to others*.

Inquiring the suppliers in this context is about asking few reliable suppliers simultaneously to quote a price and its technical proposal to do your work but reminding the supplier that he is competing with other suppliers to do the work. This will make the supplier to give his best price, delivery period or quality work to win the bid. Asking few reliable suppliers will also enable you to turn to other supplier promptly if one of the supplier turn down your offer.

However, you have to demonstrate that you have the capability to reward them if you want them to bid for the work by either one or the combination of the following, whichever is practical and effective to you at that point of time:

- Indicating your potential customers who are good paymaster or demonstrating your wealth;
- Indicating the opportunities to prove and market themselves, to gain valuable experience and to do other opportunity work;
- Offering your supplier to become the shareholder of your high profit margin business.

You may inquire from the suppliers the following information with respect to their product/service:
- Track record showing clearly the scope of work, client, value and date;
- Application and benefit compared to their competitor (**life cycle cost**, inter-changeability of parts to existing product, warranty/ guarantee, etc.);
- Concerns and how it is being addressed;
- Work process to prepare, operate and maintain the product and the associated rates/prices, productivity, quality test method, SHE certain precaution;
- List of sub-suppliers (**original suppliers**) and **special tools/ equipment**;
- Other alternative products;
- Suppliers' contact tel., fax., e-mail, address.

Then, you may check with the supplier's other clients to confirm the supplier's performance, product application, benefit and concerns. You may also ask that client if he want to order the product/service again and you make the offer to order for them. You may later ask the supplier for a discount for making a big combined order with that client.

Normally those supplier which is technically acceptable and quoting the lowest bid price will be awarded the work. But you may conduct negotiation before awarding the work.

The aim of the negotiation should be a win-win to both parties for long term benefit. You do not want the supplier to make a loss or ask for ridiculous discount because it can give negative effect on you i.e. the supplier may either do short cut to complete the work, give you substandard product or quit in the middle of the work.

You may negotiate either one or the combination of the following, whichever is practical and effective to you at that point of time and whichever is agreeable to the supplier:

- From the proposed work process to prepare the product/service and the associated rates/prices and productivity, take out from the supplier those work process/area where it can be done cheaper/faster by owned or other cheaper supplier. In this context, you **ask the suppliers to work together** by dividing the work by work area such that the total price will be cheaper or the total duration will be shorter than if it would be done by one supplier but there should be less interfacing problem. This arrangement will also enable prompt mobilization and taking over by the supplier in case of nonperformance of other supplier, **simultaneous** action by all suppliers and cross quality audit among suppliers;
- Performance bond in term of retention money or bank guarantee to assure that the supplier will not quit before completing the work, to make good the product if found defective during the warranty period and as a start up capital (in case of retention money) for you to manage the work;
- **Target to complete the work earlier** and apply LAD (Liquidated Ascertain Damage). LAD is a kind of penalty that the supplier has to pay if the work delay, normally in the form of deduction from the contract price;

- Do additional work without additional cost e.g. training, doing other work which is located nearby/at the supplier's work site.

You may negotiate such that there will be zero out-of-pocket money for you by the following:

- You will pay the supplier after receiving the payment from your customer or after receiving the loans/claims by asking favorable credit terms from your supplier e.g. 45 days payment term or pay your supplier after expiry of the warranty/guarantee period;
- Payment by barter trading i.e. by giving your product/ service to your supplier;
- **Cost/reward sharing**;
- **Middling**.

If the above fail, you may go to the supplier who is quoting the second lowest price but still technically acceptable. If this fail too, then you go on with other suppliers.

For example, you want to renovate your house. So you ask few contractors to give their technical proposals and price for the work. From the technical proposal, you find out that Contractor A, B and C is technically acceptable after confirming with their previous clients. Among the three contractors, Contractor B quote the lowest price. So you negotiate with Contractor B.

From the work processes, you find out that the ceiling work is the most expensive. So you tell Contractor B to exclude the ceiling work and reduce the price accordingly. You find out that Contractor A quote very low for the ceiling work, though Contractor A quote higher than Contractor B in the overall renovation work, so you plan to award the ceiling work to Contractor A.

Then you ask Contractor B to consider the following:

- To reduce the completion time but you will apply LAD, say 2% of the contract price per day of delay, subject to a maximum of 10% of the contract price;
- To give credit terms i.e. payment within 2 month after completion, after your renovation loan is approved;
- Since you can do welding work, you tell Contractor B that you will pay him by doing welding work at Contractor B's workshop based on the agreed rates;
- You ask Contractor B to cut the long grass at your house compound free of charge while doing the renovation work.

If Contractor B does not agree, then you tell Contractor B that you will make the offer to other contractors and so on and so on.

The problem of **asking the specialist** is that the process takes time. Therefore you may ask the specialist to do it on as-and-when required but on long term basis i.e. to quote in unit rates (apart from the lump sum price) that will cover the work plus other anticipated works in the future and the unit rates be valid for a long term. This will make this time consuming process be applicable to future works and therefore you will not repeat the whole process all over again in the future.

The other potential problem of **asking the specialist** is that you may depend on them too much or no specialist may want to work for you. So from the given work process, list of sub-suppliers (**original suppliers**) and list of tools/equipment, you may **learn, teach others (those who will do the work for you fast and cheap) and acquire the resources to do** the wholesome specialist work by ourselves or by **prepared/owned/local resources** at certain part where;

- **Life cycle cost** of acquiring the special tool and other associated resources is lower than asking the specialist to do the work or;
- Mobilization time of the specialist is not acceptable for such critical service or;
- Asking others to do the work will expose them to your confidential/secret matters;
- It will add value to your skill and knowledge.

Otherwise, from the list of alternatives product given by suppliers, you pursue with other alternatives.

Learn

One of the thing that differentiate man and animal is the ability to learn. Man progress much more than animal because man can learn better than animal. While among men, those who can learn faster and better will have bigger potential to be more successful than the others.

What to learn? For a problem, you want to know minimally what is the risk of doing nothing, where/when is it critical, what are the possible causes, what is the root cause (what is the work that caused the problem). For a solution, you want to know minimally what is the application, what are the processes, what are the productivity level (quantity of work per unit time) and unit rates for each process, what are the conditions for it to work, what are the other alternatives, who are the suppliers and clients.

How to learn fast? Learning by comparing with the one thing that you know very well may make the learning process faster. If you are walking in a big city and you try to remember your way back to your hotel by remembering which streets that you had passed, you may lose your way because you have to remember so many streets and so many lefts and rights. But if you remember the one tall building which is nearer to your hotel, then you may only need to look at that one tall building to find your hotel.

If you try to learn the various types of welding processes by remembering all the information with respect to the welding processes, then you may take a longer learning time. But if you remember just one welding process and you learn the other welding processes by remembering only the things which differentiate them, the learning process may be faster.

If you try to explain to uneducated smokers of the distance in kilometers, you may have difficult task to explain what is kilometer all about. But if you say that the distance is about taking five cigarettes if he walk on foot, then he may better understand the distance.

Another way of learning is by remembering the initial letter and make a word out of the long texts. Your wife ask you to buy sugar, egg, apple, beef, orange, lamb chop. All you need to remember is **sea bol**, then you will remember the whole list of things to buy.

Another way of learning is to quickly recite what you have learned. You read an article. After reading, you recite what you have read and check again whether what you have recited is correct and recite again until you remember the whole thing.

If you read something, you will involve your eyes to learn. If you go to a classroom, you will involve your eyes and ears to learn. If you do the thing, you may involve all your five senses to learn (eyes, ears, hands, nose and tongue). So far, learning by doing is acknowledged the best way to learn. It is the fastest way to store what you have learned into your permanent memory.

Learning by **teaching others** is another effective way to learn. When you teach others, you will get the feedback/questions that will reinforce your learning. To the writer, teaching others is the **next definite step** of learning. So you may teach others immediately on what you have learned and then you take the opportunity of the feedback/questions to review and practice what you have learned.

Teach Others

You do the work yourself and get the knowledge of doing it. Then you **teach others** to complete the work with the knowledge that you had. Then these people will, in turn, after doing the work, teach the others to do similar work and so on and so on. This is normally done by **cost/reward sharing**. This is called chain reaction.

Chain reaction will cause an initially small effort by yourself to finally yield big result in a short time. However, chain reaction will only be applicable to work of similar nature.

You had a big family and one servant. After dinner, your servant will be spending hours on dish washing. Your only one servant need to do other important things too. So you try to help your servant by at least removing the unwanted dish from your plate into the rubbish bin. Then you teach your elder children to do this simple work too. Then, in turn, your elder children teach your younger children to do this simple work. Imagine the time saving on dish washing that can be achieved.
The problem with **teach others** is that what you want them to do may not be exactly what you want as it pass from one hand

to many other hands. So you may record what you want to maintain its originality and you also ask for suggestion to improve it as you pass it to others.

The meaning of the terms used so far in Chapter 2 are as follows:

Life Cycle Cost

A **life cycle cost** of a product is the net present value (NPV) of the product after considering the cost of acquisition, cost of sustaining (operation and maintenance) during its useful life and cost of decommissioning (phasing out, disposal).

A product may be expensive to buy but after considering the cost of operation and maintenance during its useful life, the **life cycle cost** may be low.

You buy battery X at 1.00 dollar and it got flat after 3 days usage. In 30 days you had bought 10 number of battery X at 10.00 dollar. But you buy battery Y at 3.00 dollar and in 30 days you had bought for two number of battery Y at 6.00 dollar. Though battery X is cheaper than battery Y but in the long run, battery X is expensive than battery Y.

Some people buy expensive things because of some other values such as reputation, "make life easy", safety, etc. But still, a strict finance guy can argue that these values can be converted into dollar and cent e.g. how much potential revenue will this reputation generate? How much potential man-hours (thus money) can be saved by this "make life easy" product? How much potential loss of revenue due to stoppages of work, potential loss of money due to compensation to the victim, potential loss of man-hours for accident investigation, potential loss of reputation and potential loss of revenue due to accident can be saved by this safe product?

To the writer, as "money is not everything", some values should not be converted into dollar and cent. You may draw a line between what is acceptable and what is not acceptable in terms of reputation (dignity, religion, custom, political belief), SHE and customer's satisfaction which the writer hereby called the product "technical acceptability". If you have the options, then you may select the product which is "technically acceptable" and the lowest **life cycle cost**.

The problem of estimating the **life cycle cost** is that the figures may not be realistic, especially when the useful life is too long. For example, nobody can forecast the price of oil accurately, especially in the far future. So you may find out when will the NPV of a product will break-even with the NPV of another product, and determine whether that break-even point is too long for the figures to be realistic.

Partial Delivery

The mistake that we normally do is to wait until the product is fully completed before we deliver to our customer. If you can deliver the product in stages/phases or make **partial delivery**;

- You will be able to get the feedback from your customer earlier and hence you would not waste your time to proceed with unnecessary work;
- You may also get partial payment from your customer for this **partial delivery**;
- It will enable your customer to proceed with his work earlier upon receiving your partial product;
- You are also seen as reporting the work progress to your customer.

This formula is derived from the philosophy *problem can be solved by solving other problem*.

The problem with **partial delivery** is that you may end up with more delivery cost. So you may ask the customer to bear the delivery cost or deliver the product when the customer visit you.

Conditions of Acceptance

Quality is about meeting customer's requirement. To the writer's perspective, it is about getting customer's acceptance to the proposed service/product.

You may deliver quality product either by;
- Option 1: Asking the customer what they want before you prepare the product;
- Option 2: Preparing the product first and later ask the customer what are the conditions for him to accept the product.

If you apply Option 1, the advantage is that you may not end up with rework but the disadvantage is that what the customer want may be beyond your capability and when the customer do not know exactly what he want or what he want is not clear, you may end up in many rework because of the changes that need to be done afterward.

If you apply Option 2, the advantage is that the product is within your capability and you may still get it accepted by asking the conditions of acceptance. The disadvantage is that the customer may not want to give any **conditions of acceptance** or the **conditions of acceptance** is beyond your capability/control.

To get the best of the two worlds, you may prepare first the product within your capability/control to certain extent (prototype, initial product, etc.) and then you ask the customer his **conditions of acceptance** and/or other special requirement before you proceed to complete the product. In this way if the customer completely reject the initial product, you will not lose so much but if he agree you would have saved much time to get your project started.

This is what many house developer do. They prepare the drawings or the model of the house based on their capability. Then they advertise for booking and getting feedback. Finally they built the actual house tailored to the customer's requirement.

The **conditions of acceptance** is the conditions stipulated by those affected by the decision in order for them to accept the decision. It is about a problem solver proposing a service/product and asking those who will be affected by the decision to tell him the condition that he need to comply in order for his service/product be accepted. This is an efficient way of getting the acceptance (and thus the quality).

The **conditions of acceptance** may be applied to solve conflicts. If two parties have different opinion on how to solve certain issue, you find out which of the opinion is practicable and ask the other party to state his conditions to accept that practicable option.

The **conditions of acceptance** may also be used as a tool for negotiation. You may propose something and ask the other party his conditions to accept your proposal.

Swapping

Swapping is about taking out the product being currently used to replace another similar defective product.

Normally, swapping can solve your problem faster than if you have to repair the defective product.

You had a defective portable fan in your bedroom but you need it urgently before you sleep that night. Instead of repairing the defective fan, you take out the portable fan from your living room to replace (swap with) the defective fan. Tomorrow you may arrange to repair the defective fan.

The problem of **swapping** is that you do more work than repairing the defective product because you still need to repair the defective product. So you do **swapping** only when it is necessary to achieve zero time.

Simultaneous

You do things **simultaneously** and thus faster if;
- You do the next steps at the same time with the current step;
- You break down the work into workable parts and you ask few workers to work the parts at the same time;
- You do all the options at the same time when you are unsure of the success of an option.

The problem of doing things **simultaneously** is that you have to engage more workers. So these workers should be able to back up/cover each other when required and be able to do other opportunity works.

Use of Prepared/Local/Owned Resources

Using prepared resources will definitely cut down setup time while using local resources will reduce mobilization cost and time.

Using owned resources will reduce the cost. Imagine if the sub-suppliers of owned resources is also owned resources, then you may get the work done free of charge. This is what businessmen tend to do; he find out how to own his major sub-supplier by becoming the shareholder of his sub-supplier or he set up a company to supply a product to his other company.

Prepared/local/owned resources have their limitations, therefore you may mix with specialist/special resources to get work done.

Special Tool

One of the reason why things can be done better and faster is because they use **special tool** or equipment. SWAT team use special weapon and tactics, NASA use **special tools**/equipment and all other great performers use special tool. Magician do not show their **special tool** when they perform so that you will think it's magic. This formula is derived from the philosophy *problem can be transferred to an object.*

Computer is a **special tool,** so is this problem solving formula. But one thing to remember about special tool is that it is only a processor. If the input is bad, the output is also bad; rubbish in, rubbish out.

Because **special tool** is special, you tend to end up with many special tools for small difficult job. Then it's time to think of one tool that has many special functions. This is **what you want ultimately** .

The other problem with **special tool** is that it is expensive to buy and maintain. So you may supply your **special tool** to your supplier in order to improve delivery period or work quality but you charge your supplier the rental rate to reduce the cost charge by your supplier.

<u>Original Supplier</u>

Getting the product directly from the **original supplier** may reduce the cost and time because you will bypass the agents/middlemen. You may also get the right quality because the product has not been diluted by other party.

The potential problem with **original supplier** is that they may not want to entertain your small request. So you may volunteer to also order for other clients and you may get a discount in your order for such big orders.

The other potential problem with **original supplier** is that you may have to depend only on them for maintenance of their product due to their contract warranty clause or unclear product's specifications/drawings. So you may ask them to supply complete product's specifications/drawings when you buy the product such that you can ask for competitive bidding for maintenance work.

Target to Complete Earlier

This is one of the way to ensure that a work will complete on time, if not completing it ahead of schedule. The following can cause delay in the work:

- Emerging work that need to be completed at the same time with planned work;
- Force majeure (very bad weather, earthquake, flood, etc.).

Giving some allowance in completion time will help to cover the above causes of delay and ensure the work complete on time.

Target to complete earlier may be applicable for big project such as getting **what you want ultimately.**

The problem of targeting to complete earlier is that you may target too early that you may sacrifice the quality to meet the schedule. So you may target to complete just 10-25% ahead of schedule.

Cost/Reward Sharing

You may share the cost and later share the reward with the supplier, the other users of the product or those who will be affected by the decision. This formula is derived from the philosophy *problem can be transferred to others*.

You may ask them to bear all the cost (therefore zero cost for you) and the reward of delivering the product/service will be shared among yourself and those who bear the cost.

You may also make the order for other users and ask the supplier a discount or even one free for you (therefore zero cost for you) for such big orders.

The problem of **cost/reward sharing** is that many people want to share the reward but not the cost. So you should have many choices of potential shareholders, able to demonstrate quick and good returns in their investment and targeting customers who are good paymaster.

The other potential problem of **cost/reward sharing** is that the reward may turn to be so big that you might think in the first place it's better for you to finance all the work by yourself and get the maximum reward. So you may specify certain share percentage to other shareholders which is subject to a maximum value of say double the cost of the product/service.

Middling

You negotiate with your supplier and you get say a 50% discount. Then you sell the product to other user at non-discounted price and you get a 50% profit. With this profit, you buy the product again for yourself. This is called **middling**.

The problem with **middling** is that you need to come out with some cash initially to buy the product. So you may find out other users/buyers first before you buy the product, ask for credit term from your supplier (say 30 or 45 days payment term) and you use the money from other users/buyers to pay your supplier.

Chapter 3 : Down To Earth

This chapter will illustrate how the formulas as explained in Chapter 2 were applied in the management of fast track projects by some reputable companies in the world. These formulas were applied in piece meal basis, not in the integrated manner, therefore they are not the best practices yet though may be claimed to be so. These formulas will be integrated in Chapter 4 to form the desired problem solving principle.

1.0 Project Initiation

The Project Initiation process normally began with the appointment of a Project Manager by company's management. With some background information of the project, the Project Manager would, in turn, formed his integrated Project Preparation Team and defined the roles and responsibilities for the preparation of the project.

The Project Preparation Team would include, primarily the following:
(a) Project Manager;
(b) Multi-discipline Planners.
Depending on the size of the project, other team members may include;
(c) Safety Officer;
(d) Scheduler;
(e) Quality Control Officer;

(f) Material Coordinator;
(g) Logistic Coordinator;
(h) Cost Control/Contract Officer;
(i) Other technical support group.

This Project Preparation Team would later constitute the core group of the Project Execution Team.

The Project Preparation Team would deliberate on the following:
(a) Project Mission; the "why" of the project;
(b) Major Work; to estimate the project execution duration and identify long lead item for planning purposes;
(c) Project Objectives w.r.t. Safety, Health & Environment (SHE), Quality, Duration/Schedule and Cost;
(d) Project Strategies, Business Processes, Plans/Procedures to meet the above Project Objectives.

Typically the Project Objectives would be as follows:

SHE   -   *Zero accident, zero environmental infringement*
Quality   -   *Zero rework*
Schedule -   On time
Cost   -   No cost overrun

Note : Here we can see that zero mistake i.e. zero accident/ environmental infringement and zero rework were already pursued. In the future, it will not be surprising for people to pursue zero time and zero cost.

Duration would be achievable and an improvement in performance from previous projects of similar work sizes and working hours/pattern.

To formulate the Project Implementation Plan, the Project Preparation Team would review;

(a) _Lessons learnt and recommendations_ from previous Project Team;
(b) Best practices by other companies;
(c) Relevant company's future plans;
(d) Future project schedule of companies who would use same contractors to avoid, wherever possible, clashes in project schedule.

Note: Here we can see **taking certain precautions** was applied; seeking lessons learnt from previous team.

Simultaneously, the Material Coordinator would request the project team to submit the tentative long lead item list for making the inquiry to potential suppliers. The purchase order would only be issued once the long lead item had been confirmed.

Note: Here we can see the **next definite step** was applied; the tentative long lead item was compiled before the project work scope was determined.

Then, the Project Manager would _prepare the Project Implementation Plan for endorsement of the management,_ highlighting the changes from previous practice, if any, which would include;
(a) Project Mission;
(b) Project Major Work;
(c) Project Objectives w.r.t. SHE, Quality, Schedule, Duration and Cost;
(d) Project Strategies;
(e) Project Business Processes;
(f) Project Plan;
(g) Project Preparation Organization;
(h) Communication Plan.

Note : Here we can see **taking precautions** was applied; making **partial delivery** (of his Project Implementation Plan) to his customer (management) for their **conditions of** *acceptance.*

The duration/schedule specified here was indicative only and meant for scheduling purposes. The precise duration/schedule would be determined after the work scope challenge process and detailed scheduling carried out.

2.0 Project Preparation

Once the Project Implementation Plan had been endorsed by the management, the Project Manager would arrange to *"sell" his Project Implementation Plan to be understood and accepted by his Project Preparation Team and others who will be directly or indirectly involved* in the preparation and execution of the project.
*Note: Here we can see **taking precautions** was applied; **teach others** (Project Preparation Team) **to complete** the work.*

The project preparation would then commence with the following activities:

2.1 Initial Work Scope

The Planner would request the work-lists generators to submit the work-lists by adhering to certain format.

The work-lists would cover all planned work, normally 90% of the total project work-lists.

The late work-lists would cover unplanned work such as ongoing defects and associated work which could only be identified after the closing date for submission of the work-lists.

The submitted work-lists would minimally indicate;
(a) Description of the work;
(b) Reason for the work;
(c) *Risk of not doing the work in this project;*
(d) *Risk of delaying the work to subsequent project*;
*Note: Here we can see review of the **criticality** was applied.*
(e) Major tools/equipment requirement;
(f) Estimated man-hours/cost.

After the closing date, the Planner would arrange to carry out a preview;
(a) To ensure that the work-lists were comprehensive as per the expected coverage;
(b) To ensure that the work-lists were not duplicating;
(c) To ensure that the submitted work-lists were duly completed as per required format and clearly written.

Then, the Planner would arrange for the Work-lists Challenge Meeting;
(a) To challenge on the "what-to-do". Is it necessary for the work to be done in this project, not the next project? A *Risk Assessment Matrix* would typically be used for this work scope challenge.
*Note: Here we can see the review on the **criticality** was applied.*
(b) To challenge on the "how-to-do". Is it "fit-for-purpose"?
(c) To challenge on the "who-to-do". What is the required competency? Is in-house manpower competent and available for the work? Will the in-house manpower add value to their skill and knowledge by doing the work? Will there be minimum work interfaces?

Once the work-lists was approved, the Planner would arrange;
(a) To compile the approved work-lists and sort according to

the work categories/discipline;
(b) A meeting for the identification of the project critical path and high cost work and subsequently finding ways to shorten the project duration and to optimize the cost.

2.2 Budget Review

Once the work-lists had been approved, the _Project Budget would be reviewed_ to ensure that the Project Budget would not only be able to cover the work-lists, but also the anticipated remaining work-lists which was about 10% of the total project work-lists. If necessary, the Project Manager would arrange to ask for supplementary budget.
Note: Here we can see the **next definite step** was applied; the budget was reviewed in the initial stage of the project than rather after physical work was done to ensure sufficient money was allocated for the project.

2.3 Final Work Scope

This list would cover up to only 10% of the total project work-lists such as ongoing defects and associated work which could only be identified after the closing date of the work-lists.

The late work-lists would be challenged in the same manner as the work-lists.

Where external service was required for the approved late work-lists, the list would be first incorporated in the contract packages of the initial work-lists, wherever possible. Otherwise, a new contract package would be prepared.

Once the late work-lists had been accepted after the work-lists challenge meeting, the late work-lists would be presented by the Work Generator for _higher management approval_, if the work could be identified earlier before the closing date of the work-lists.

At the discretion of the Project Manager, depending on the size and complexity of the work, the preparation and execution of the approved late work-lists would be handled by a _separate team_ but coordinated by the Project Preparation/ Execution Team.

Note: Here we can see the handling of **remaining part of the problem** (the late work-lists) by **asking the specialist** (higher management to approve the late work-lists and separate team to prepare/execute the work).

The purposes of the late work-lists system were to;
(a) Discourage late work inclusion by Work-lists Generator;
(b) Avoid rush orders which would normally incurred higher cost;
(c) Control contract variation orders;
(d) Ensure adequate preparation and supervision for execution of the late work-lists.

Once the project execution commenced, any new work request would be known as extra/additional work. All such work would be approved in the same manner as the late work-lists. However, for fast track project, a dedicated team which would be readily available be set up to quickly evaluate the extra/ additional work for approval of the Project Manager in order to avoid delay in the approval process.

2.4 Contract Preparation

If you had prepared a good contract; prepared a good contract strategy and selected good contractor, then you have won half of the battle to manage a project.

The processes for the preparation of the contract were as follows:

2.4.1 Contract Strategy

As soon as the work-lists had been approved, a Contract Strategy and the Bidders' List would be prepared by work-lists generator or end-users for work which would require use of external service.

The Contract Strategy would be presented for endorsement of the Tender Committee which minimally cover the following:

(a) Reasons for requiring the contract
Typical reasons were;
- Inadequate in-house resources;
- Specialist work;
- Work which would not add value to the skill and knowledge of in-house manpower;

(b) Mode of tendering
Typically the mode of tendering were;
- Closed tender to company's registered contractors;
- Open tender;
- Negotiation with selected contractors.

(c) Type of contract
Typically the type of contract in a project would be a lump

sum contract as majority of the work could be clearly defined. The use of the lump sum contract would enable control of project cost as the price of the work had been predetermined before start of work. However, anticipated emergent work would be highlighted to contractor so that the contractor would be better prepared should it occur. This emergent work would be paid by variation order as per agreed rates for variation work in that lump sum contract. The use of unit rates or reimbursable contract in a well defined project was avoided as far as practicable as there was no incentive for the contractor to reduce the work duration.

(d) Project Work Schedule
The project work schedule would be a baseline schedule. Bidders were required to submit detailed schedule.

(e) Terms of payment
Typically there will be a Progressive Payment Scheme to enable the contractor to finance the project work and thus the contractor would be able to perform as expected.

The progressive payment was typically made upon;
- award of contract;
- mobilization of contractor's resources at site;
- certain percentage of work completion;
- completion and acceptance of work.

Due to the short duration of a fast track project, progressive payment must be made timely, otherwise it would defeat the purpose.

(f) Bid bond
Bid bond was required to discourage the successful bidder to withdraw after the contract was awarded.

(g) Performance bond
Performance bond was required to discourage the contractor to withdraw during work execution and to ensure that any rework after initial acceptance would be attended. Bid bond would normally be released after receipt of the performance bond.

(h) Liquidated Ascertained Damage (LAD)
*Note: Here we can see **ask the supplier** was applied.*

(i) Others
Insurance and schedule of contract preparation process.

Bidders' List

Bidders were selected as follows:

(a) Closed tender
Bidders were company's registered contractors with relevant experience and acceptable performance. Only if the registered list was inadequate for competitive bidding, then the tender would also be opened to other contractors with relevant experience and acceptable performance. These other contractors would be asked to apply for registration with the company before award of contract .

(b) Negotiation with selected contractors
These selected contractors could either be the OEM (original equipmentmanufacturer) or certain contractors that hold an exclusive license. In case of the OEM, you may have to get their service for the first few years for maintenance work, otherwise they would not give you the product warranty.

Incentive-based Contract

There were times when earlier completion of the project with good quality and safety performance would increase company's income/profitability significantly. Under such circumstances, to enhance contractor's performance, an incentive in terms of bonus would be considered for deserving contractor.

Note : Here we can see ask the specialist was applied; bonus, a kind of reward sharing was offered to contractors.

A typical formula of the bonus was as follows:

$$B = P \times I \times D \times Q \times S$$

Where;

B = Bonus

P = Cumulative contract price (including variation order, if any)

I = Investment Rate (e.g. bank fixed deposit rate)

D = Duration factor

= 1	if Actual Duration/Contractual Duration < 0.6	
= 0.9		> 0.5
= 0.8		> 0.6
= 0.7		> 0.7
= 0.6		> 0.8
= 0	if equal or behind schedule	

Q = Quality factor
  = 1   if no rework after hand-over
  = 0.5 if rework after hand-over but with no impact on overall project schedule
  = 0   if rework after hand-over and affect overall project schedule

S = Safety factor
- = 1   if no Lost Time Incident (LTI), Medical Treatment Case (MTC), Minor First Aid (MFA), property damage, environmental infringement occur
- = 0   if any LTI, MTC, MFA, property damage, environmental infringement occur

The formulas above would encourage the contractors to perform in terms of time, quality and safety but also ensure that the contractor would not receive more than certain amount i.e. certain percentage of the contract price; this percentage could be bank's fixed deposit rate.

However, Contractor shall accept variation order without any change to the planned schedule/duration.

<u>Example</u>

Contractor XYZ successfully completed the work 2 days ahead of schedule. The contractual work duration is 10 days. There was some rework after work hand-over but the rework did not affect the overall project schedule. There was no incident during work execution. The value of the contract was 700,000 dollars and the value of variation order was 100,000 dollars.

Hence;

P   = Cumulative contract price is 800,000 dollars

I   = Investment Rate is 5 % = 0.05

D   = Duration factor
    = 0.7 as Actual Duration/Contractual Duration = 0.8

Q   = Quality factor
    = 0.5 as rework after hand-over but with no impact on overall project schedule

S   = Safety factor

= 1 as no LTI, MTC, MFA, property damage

Therefore, the bonus;
B   = P x I x D x Q x S
          = 800,000 x 0.05 x 0.7 x 0.5 x 1
          = 11,200 dollars

2.4.2 Invitation-To-Bid Documents (ITB)

The ITB would be prepared in parallel with the Contracting Strategy and Bidders' List.

The following were typical contents of the ITB:
(a) Invitation-to-Tender Letter;
(b) Secrecy Undertaking;
(c) Instruction to Tenderer;
(d) Form of Tender;
(e) Statement of Compliance Form;
(f) Statement of Qualification/Deviation;
(g) General Conditions of Contract;
(h) Draft Agreement.

Any deviations in the contents for the above were made in consultation with company's legal personnel and highlighted to the respective Tender Committee.

The following contents of the ITB were customized to work requirement:

(a) Work Specifications
Typical contents of the Work Specifications were;
- Contractor's Scope of Work/Supply;
- Technical Specification;
- Company's Scope of Supply;

- Work Schedule & Duration.

(b) Quotation Form/Schedule of Rates
For a lump sum contract, the Quotation Form would be breakdown into manpower, material and tools/equipment and specifically stating the quantities and unit rates to facilitate the technical or commercial evaluation of the bid.

The format of the Quotation Form must be line with the format of company's Cost Estimate to enable apple-to-apple comparison during the commercial evaluation exercise.

The Schedule of Rates for Variation Order or for unit rate contract would be prepared for anticipated emergent work so that there will be no dispute in the price for variation work in the project.

(c) Technical information to be submitted by bidders
Bidders were requested to submit the following information in their bid:
- *Track record*;
- Resume of key personnel;
- *List of tools/equipment*;
- Work schedule;
- *Quality Plan;*
- *SHE Plan;*
- Implementation Plan;
- Organization Chart & Manpower loading;
- *Work procedures;*
- *List of sub-suppliers;*
- *Alternative bid*, if any. However, bidders' alternative bid would not be considered if bidder had not submitted the base bid.
Note: Here we can see **ask the suppliers** was applied.

2.4.3 Issuance of ITB

Ample time would be given to bidders to understand and submit their tenders .

A Site Visit session would be conducted with the bidders to;
- clarify any queries w.r.t. the ITB;
- familiarize bidders with the work site and available facilities to be supplied by company during the project execution.

Any changes to the scope or clarification by company as a result of the site visit would be communicated to all the bidders. Any changes of the scope would warrant review of the Cost Estimate.

The Site Visit would be conducted such that the bidders would not be able to know their competitors.

The tender would be submitted in two separate sealed envelope, i.e.;
(a) Technical Proposal;
(b) Commercial Proposal.

The technical proposal would be opened first. Once the technical proposal have been evaluated then only the commercial proposal were opened. The reasons for not opening the two proposals simultaneously were;
- To avoid a bias evaluation on the technical proposal once the price was known;
- To be fair with all the bidders. The bidders were given the chance to amend their price as a result of clarification during the technical evaluation. If the price of all the bidders were known, then the price could be made known to the favored bidder so that favored bidder could amend his price to be the

lowest bidder and won the contract.

However, *for contract of lower value, simultaneous opening* of the technical and commercial proposal would be practiced. *Note: Here we can see **simultaneous action** was applied at selected part.*

2.4.4 Technical Evaluation

Before the bidders' Technical Proposal were opened, the Technical Evaluation Criteria and the list of tender evaluation team (Technical Evaluation Team and Commercial Evaluation Team) would be prepared by the end-users for endorsement of the respective Tender Committee.

The Technical Evaluation Criteria would be prepared after the Tender Closing date and time to ensure that the Technical Evaluation Criteria was not made known to the bidders.

The Project Manager (apart from the end-users and the discipline specialist) *would normally be the member of the Tender Evaluation Team of the major contract packages* to;
- resolve issues that were common to the evaluation team of different project contract packages to avoid double standards;
- alert other evaluation team members of possible same contractors' key personnel for different project contract packages;
- notify other evaluation team members of possible changes in project plan that may affect the evaluation of the tender;
- coordinate the plan to interview the contractors' key personnel if required.
*Note: Here we can see **at certain part, do it by ourselves** (Project Manager) was applied.*

Bidders would be requested to submit their technical clarification under the following circumstances:
- Uncertainties in the bidders' Technical Proposal;
- Deviation in the bidders' Technical Proposal from company's estimate such as manpower loading, material bill of quantities and equipment loading. Care would be taken to ensure that the actual company's estimate were not revealed to the bidders unless the estimate were specifically mentioned in the ITB.

As the competency of bidders' manpower was one of the main criteria to be evaluated, an interview session/trade test would be conducted, especially when the person has never worked in company's site/environment yet to;
- Verify their resume/curriculum vitae;
- Test their proficiency in communication especially for those who will be handling Work Permits such as Work Leaders/ Foremen/Supervisor;
- Ensure their availability during the project.

Bidders would also be asked to submit _details of alternative personnel with mobilization plan_ for pre-evaluation to assure the manpower was adequate should the;
- Existing manpower be pinched by other contractor;
- Existing manpower did not perform or breaching company's rules/regulations;
- Work delay due to inadequate manpower;
- Existing crew was tired at the end of project.
Note: Here we can see **taking certain precautions** was applied; increasing **what we have/can** (list of contractor's manpower) to ensure adequacy of manpower.

A database of contractors' manpower who have worked in the company would normally be created and updated to facilitate the technical evaluation of bidders' proposed manpower.

All technical queries must be done and clarified in this technical evaluation stage as technical queries were not allowed during the commercial evaluation stage.

The bidders were also allowed to submit cost impact as a result of the technical clarification in a sealed envelope and to be opened only during the commercial evaluation stage.

The Technical Evaluation Team would later prepare the Technical Evaluation Report for endorsement of the respective Tender Committee.

2.4.5 Commercial Evaluation

Once the Technical Evaluation Report has been endorsed by the respective Tender Committee, then the Commercial Proposal of the technically acceptable bidders would be opened.

There would be no communication with bidders. Under certain circumstances where communication with bidders was inevitable (such as to confirm the pricing due to typing error, etc.), the approval to communicate with the bidders would be obtained from the respective Tender Committee .

The sensitivities of the unit rates for variation order would be analyzed to obtain an overall pricing of the bidders.

Award would be based on the concept of "technically acceptable, lowest bidder".

Pre-award negotiation with the lowest bidder would be conducted if its price was much higher than company's

estimate. As it's unfair to ask the lowest bidder to reduce the price (unfair because the request to reduce the price should be made to all bidders), the lowest bidder would normally be asked to *do additional work without increasing its existing price*.
*Note : Here we can see **ask the supplier** was applied.*

2.5 Material Preparation

2.5.1 Material Requisition/Reservation

Upon receipt of the Material List, the Material Coordinator would arrange to finalize the Material List for procurement after considering the;
(a) Quantities of material used in the past similar project such as by reviewing the Material Control Sheet of the past projects;
(b) Basis of the ordered quantities, i.e. the actual required and the contingency quantities;
(c) Stock level where company keep stock.

2.5.2 Material Receipt & Storage

For fast track project, the following material would be stored at *Project Material Cabin near to work site* to minimize lost of man-hours in collecting and transporting the material to the work site:
(a) Fast moving material;
(b   Material which did not require special storage condition;
(c) Inexpensive material;
(d) Light weight and not bulky material.
*Note : Here we can see use of **what we have/can** was*

applied; use of local resources (cabin local to work site).

Other materials would be stored in the Material Warehouse which was far from the work site.

2.5.3 Material Tracking

The Material Coordinator would coordinate material tracking activities to monitor the status of all project material and carry out expediting work, if required. A report would be prepared on regular basis to show the status from the initial requisition up to issue and return of material.

2.5.4 Material Issuance

A Material Control Sheet would be prepared to control issuance and return of material.

Issuance would be done progressively such as one day before use so that the contractor would not store excessive material in their cabin and later lead to problem of trace-ability.

For certain maintenance project, material would be issued based on the "issue new for old" concept. The purposes of the "issue new for old" concept were to ;
(a) Confirm the material which were intended for "like- for- like" replacement;
(b) Avoid unnecessary issuance of material should the actual material required varies from the material listed in the Material Control Sheet;
(c) Improve housekeeping as old material would be removed from site promptly.

2.6 Logistic

Logistic activities, a commonly underestimated activities, were equally important to ensure smooth project execution work.

Logistic activities would include preparation (and post activities) for;
(a) Project Village;
(b) Tools/equipment/cabin lay-down area at work site;
(c) Common tools/equipment to be supplied to contractors;
(d) Communication facilities such as walkie-talkies, radios, etc.;
(e) Sales of scrap metal;
(f) Other support services as requested by Project Manager.

(a) Project Village

A Project Village, near to the work site would be set up to monitor and coordinate the work of contractors.

The Project Village would comprise minimally the following:
Note: Here e will see what we have/can were provided to contractors in order to save time and cost.

(ai) Site Offices
Site Offices, typically port a-cabins would be prepared for the Project Team (both company and contractors) to facilitate work progress monitoring and coordination of work.

(aii) Fabrication Yard
A Fabrication Yard was provided for contractors' use in the Project Village. These facilities were provided mainly to;
- Avoid lost of man-hours and damage of company's asset if it was to be transported out and later into company's premises;

- Avoid surplus material as a result of fabrication work to be taken away by contractors if the material is supplied by company;
- Facilitate company's Quality Control Team to assess contractors' workmanship.

(aiii) Project Canteen
To minimize lost of man-hours during the project execution, contractors' personnel are required to consume their meals at the Project Canteen provided by company.

(aiv) Portable Toilets
Portable toilets would be set up at designated locations such that the toilets are easily accessible whenever required. With respect to health and environment, waste disposal, chemical treatment and supply of toilet paper rolls are deemed as essential daily activities.

(av) Parking of Vehicles
To ensure smooth flow of traffic at Project Village, a designated parking space for vehicles would be set up at the Project Village.

(avi) Muster Point
A Muster Point would be set up at the Project Village for assembly during emergencies. A signboard would be clearly displayed at the Muster Point.

(avii) Status Board
The Status Board would be set up to display key information such as overall work progress, main finding and concerns, SHE performance, etc.

(b) Common tools/equipment to be supplied to contractors
The Logistic Coordinator would arrange that the common

tools/equipment to be supplied to contractors would be in good working condition before the project execution work commence. A checklist would be prepared to record the issuance and the return of the tools/equipment.

The Material Coordinator would record those tools/equipment that are short in quantities;
- for procurement/fabrication purpose or;
- to be supplied by contractors in the future.

Contractor shall arrange to make good or replace for any lost or damaged tools/equipment while in their custody.

(c) Walkie-talkies
As timely communication was vital in fast track project, adequate walkie-talkies would be prepared for the Project Team. A dedicated Project Communication Channel would be established and common to both company and key contractors' personnel.

(d) Clearing of scrap metal
As much scrap metal would be generated in a project, the existing scrap metal must be cleared to cater for the incoming scrap metal. The Logistic Coordinator would arrange with Material Department to clear (by selling) the scrap metals before the project execution commence.

2.7 Project Execution Plan

Preparation of Project Execution Plan include preparation of;
(a) SHE Plan;
(b) Quality Plan;
(c) Engineering Plan;

(d) Information Catalogue.

(a) SHE Plan

The SHE Plan would cover topics such as;
- SHE Objectives;
- SHE Theme;
- SHE Responsibilities;
- SHE Awareness;
- Permit To Work System;
- SHE Audit & Sampling;
- Job Safety Analysis;
- Accident Reporting & Investigation;
- Emergency Response Plan;
- Waste Handling;
- Safety Procedure Guides.

(b) Quality Plan

(bi) Management Responsibility

The Project Manager, being one of the management representative would ensure that the Quality Plan were documented, understood and implemented at all levels of the Project Organization.

The roles/responsibility of the Project Team who perform work that affect quality would be defined.

The Quality Plan would be reviewed, after each project during the Lessons Learnt session to ensure its continuing suitability and effectiveness.

(bii) Quality Planning/Control

Quality planning of the work would be demonstrated in the

Job Method Sheets.

Quality control in execution of work would be achieved through use of Quality Control Sheets which would clearly indicate the work processes, hold/witness points, inspection recommendation and certification of work completion.

Quality planning would consider use of specialist contractor for certain work.

Work completion during the project would be certified by use of Initial and Final Hand-over Certificate before hand-over commence.

(biii) Contract Review

As a result of the Initial Work Scope or Final Work Scope, the planned duration or schedule of the project may have to be changed. Such change would be approved by the management, documented and communicated to all the Project Team.

(biv) Document Control

The following documents were deemed to be essential to ensure quality of work:
- Job Method Sheets;
- Material Control Sheets;
- Quality Control Sheets.

The Project Area Coordinators would ensure that only original copies were referred to when carrying out a work. Non-original copies, if referred to, must bear the "Certified Original Copy" stamp to be signed by the Project Quality Assurance Officer.

Any changes to the above document during Project Execution would be approved by the Project Manager, in consultation with the Project Technical Team.

(bv) Control of company-supplied-tools/equipment

Contractor would show documented procedures for the verification, storage and maintenance of the tools/equipment supplied by company during project.

Tools/equipment which were lost, damaged or unsuitable for use would be recorded and reported to company.

(bvi) Inspection and testing

Inspection of work during the project were guided by the Quality Control Sheets such as Welding Control Sheets, Pressure Test Certificate, Painting Inspection request, etc.

Inspection findings and recommendations were stated promptly, briefly and concisely in the above documents to enable prompt execution of the next work process. Full inspection findings and recommendations were stated in the Inspection Reports which would be issued before hand-over within the project period.

(bvii) Control of nonconforming product

Nonconforming product were reworked to meet the specified requirement before hand-over unless specified otherwise by the Project Manager.

Nonstandard repair went through company's nonstandard repair procedure.

(bviii) Corrective and preventive action

Any nonconformance detected during the project were recorded and highlighted during the various project meeting for corrective and preventive action.

Lessons Learnt session, after the project was another forum to discuss the corrective and preventive action.

(c) Engineering Plan

The Engineering Plan include ;
(i) Job Method Sheets;
(ii) Material Control Sheet.

(ci) Job Method Sheet (JMS)

This was a document to exhibit the work process, materials/ spares and tools/equipment required, man-hours and other information to facilitate the execution of a particular work.

(d) Information Catalogue

The Information Catalogue would be prepared to provide the Project Team and contractors with general information during the Project Execution. This document contain the following:
* Mission Statement;
* Premises;
* Key Performance Indicator;
* Scope of Work;
* Project Execution Organization;
* SHE Plan / Program;
* Schedule;
* Logistics;

- General Information;
  - ✓ Meeting Schedule;
  - ✓ List of Contract;
  - ✓ Telephone Numbers.

2.8 Asset Development

Asset development would comprise the following activities:
(a) *Training* of the Project Team;
(b) *Procurement* of tools/equipment;
(c) Audit of project preparation work.
*Note : Here we can see **teach others and acquire the resources** was applied.*

(a) Training of Project Team

Training of Project Team was important to ensure all personnel were competent to deliver the required service.

This training typically include;
(ai) Classroom training
- Briefing of the Project Implementation Plan;
- Visit to other companies to acquire best project practices;
- Project Workshop;
- Relevant management and technical courses.
(aii) On-the-job training
- Assignment to same/other company's project work.

On-the-job training was considered the most effective means of training.

However, such training would be implemented cautiously so as not to jeopardize the progress of the project.

On the job trainees would be working under direct supervision of experienced personnel and working on lesser critical assignment. Once those trainees have proven to be reliable, then only those trainees will be assigned a more challenging work in the next project.

To some extent, the on-the-job training also resolve the problem of unavailability of experienced personnel to fulfill certain position in the project organization.

<u>(b) Procurement of tools/equipment</u>

The adequacy and suitability of the tools/equipment to be supplied <u>to</u> contractors during the project execution would be critically reviewed.

The tools/equipment would be bought, not rented if the life cycle cost was cheaper.

<u>(c) Audit</u>

Audit was important to ensure adequacy of the Project Implementation Plan and compliance of the project preparation work to the Project Implementation Plan.
*Note : Here we can see **taking certain precautions** was applied; audit/check on its compliance to what was planned.*

Audit would be conducted by independent party to the Project Team to ensure that the assessment was not biased and to get external perspective of the project preparation work.

<u>(ci) First Audit</u>

The scope of the First Audit would be to;

- Check adequacy of the Project Implementation Plan based on auditor's perspective;
- Check compliance of the following to the Project Implementation Plan:
  - ✓ Awareness of the Project Team to the Project Implementation Plan;
  - ✓ First Work-lists;
  - ✓ Budget, cost monitoring and control;
  - ✓ ITB documents;
  - ✓ Long lead items list and First Material List.

All nonconformance detected in the First Audit will be recorded, discussed and to be closed/made good before the Second Audit.

(cii) Second Audit

The scope of the Second Audit would be to;
- Check closing of the nonconformance detected in the First Audit;
- Check compliance of the following to the Project Implementation Plan:
  - ✓ Late Work-lists;
  - ✓ Late Material List;
  - ✓ Logistic work;
  - ✓ Project Execution Plan;
  - ✓ Asset Development.

All nonconformance detected during the Second Audit would be recorded, discussed and to be closed/made good before the Pre-Project Activities commence.

2.9 Scheduling & Costing

For fast track project, work would be carried out seven days a week, including Public Holiday(s) for ten (10) hours with one (1) hour lunch break.

Depending on the criticality of the work and the actual work progress, certain work may;
- not proceed during Public Holidays;
- proceed as per normal Company work hours;
- require 24-hours work on shift cycle;
- require overtime work.

The planned duration would be shorter than all previous projects of similar critical path and work size.

The schedule would not coincide with national festivals and the project schedule of neighboring companies.

Project Management Software, typically _Primavera P3 Software tool, Timeline, Microsoft_ would be used to produce the project work schedule.

The schedule would show key activity duration, early start and late starting dates, early finish and late finish dates, total and free float and the critical path activities. Progress of main activities will be produced in S-curve.
Note : Here we can see **taking certain precautions** was applied; use of special tool (planning software).

2.9.1 Project Preparation Schedule

The Project Preparation Schedule would indicate the schedule for all the Project Business Processes from initiation of project to project close-out.

2.9.2 Project Execution Schedule

The Project Execution Schedule would be prepared upon approval of the work-lists and subsequently updated after approval of the late Work-lists.

This schedule would show detailed work plans of the project execution activities.

All initial inspection work should be scheduled to complete by half of the duration to provide adequate time for repair work, if any.

A meeting would be arranged by the Project Scheduler 3.5 months before the project execution to _seek means to shorten the critical path duration_ and hence the project execution duration without jeopardizing safety and quality.
Note : Here we can see **taking certain precautions** was applied to shorten the project execution duration such as use of special tool, arranging simultaneous activities, use of specialist service, etc.

2.9.3 Detailed Cost Estimating

Once the Invitation-To-Bid (ITB) has been prepared, the detailed cost estimate for the respective contract will be prepared by the end-users and reviewed by the Project Cost Control Officer.

The Project Cost Control Officer would ensure that the;
- Rates (manpower, equipment) were standardized;
- Quantities (manpower loading , equipment loading) were fit-for-purpose w.r.t. the project schedule such as by comparing to the standard productivity figures.

Therefore, the creation and updating of the database for project rates and productivity figures was important to make a realistic cost estimate.

2.9.4 Cost Control

The Project Cost Control Officer would exercise cost control by *challenging* end-users on the;
- *Requirement of external service* during the Work-lists Challenge Meeting;
*Note: Here we can see use **what we have/can** was pursued.*
- Clarity of ITBs such that contractors will not put too much contingencies in their pricing;
- Bidders List such that contracts undergo *competitive bidding* process;
*Note: Here we can see **ask the suppliers** was pursued.*
- Allowance in quantities of material to be ordered such that expensive material should not have too much allowance during the Material Challenge Meeting;
- Requirement of Late/Emergent/Additional Work-lists during the Work-lists Challenge Meeting;
- Requirement to hire or buy tools/equipment.

2.10 Pre-Project Execution Activities

Pre-Project activities would commence typically 45 days

before the project execution start work date, which include;

(i)   Contract Kick Off Meeting;
(ii)   *Safety Induction;*
(iii)   *Permit To Work course;*
(iv)   Job Safety Analysis;
(v)   *Briefing;*
(vi)   Permit To Work preparation;
(vii)   Tools/Equipment Inspection;
(viii)   Team Building.

Note : Here we can see **teach others** was applied.

Briefing

Pre-project briefing include briefing of the Project Execution Plan to company and contractors' personnel.

Tools/Equipment Inspection

Contractor's tools/equipment shall be inspected, tested and certified safe-for-use.

Certificates or stickers or marking will be prominently displayed at the tools/equipment to certify that the tools/ equipment were safe-for-use.

Tools/equipment that failed the test would be prevented from entering work sites.

Team Building

Teamwork among contractors & company's personnel was vital to ensure the success of the project.

A team-building program would be conducted for contractors and company's personnel such that the participants will be able to understand and apply the team-building concept and became an effective project team to meet the objectives of the project.

*Note: Here we can see **ask the specialist to work together** was pursued.*

3.0 Project Execution

(i) The Routine

Time	Activity	Personnel
Morning	Arrival of Day Shift who issue Work Permit	Client's rep.
	Hand-over of night activities	Night Supervisor Day Supervisor Area Coordinator
Morning	Arrival of Day shift	Day Shift
	Issue permit for the day work	Client's rep. Work Supervisor Work Leader
Morning	Tool Box Talk Brief on work for the day	Work Leader All tradesmen
Morning	Site work commence	All tradesmen
Morning	Daily Coordination Meeting	Project Manager Coordinators Safety Officer Scheduler Quality Officer Security Technical Team Management rep.
Morning	Technical Team Meeting (immediately after the Daily Coordination Meeting, if required)	Project Manager Technical Team Area Coordinator
	Prepare Daily Newsletter	Scheduler
Morning	Tea Break	All personnel
Morning	Site work resume	All tradesmen
Morning	Quality Audit	Quality Audit Team
Morning	Issue Daily Newsletter	Scheduler
Afternoon	Lunch Break	All personnel
Afternoon	Site work resume	All tradesmen
Afternoon	SHE Audit	SHE Audit Team
Afternoon	Tea Break	All personnel
Afternoon	Site work resume	All tradesmen
	Report on SHE, quality issues, work progress	Area Coordinator Work Supervisor
Afternoon	Report on SHE , quality issues, work progress Overtime request Punch-list (commence at mid duration)	Project Manager Area Coordinator Contractor's rep.
Afternoon	Progress Update Material Cost Update	Scheduler Area Coordinator Material Controller
	Submit work permit for tomorrow's work	Work Leader Work Supervisor Client's rep
Night	Arrival of Night Shift	Night Shift personnel
	Hand-over of day activities	Day Supervisor Night Supervisor
Night	Dinner Break and night work commence	All personnel

*Note : Here we can see **what we have/can** was applied i.e. using a fixed schedule to manage the day-to-day work.*

As work completed at certain area, the _Initial Hand-over Certificate was submitted to client's representative_, with punch list that will enable the client to commission the area. The client's representative would also arrange to carry out their own punch listing .

*Note : Here we can see **taking precautions** was applied; making **partial delivery** (Initial Hand-over Certificate) to his customer (client's representative) for their **conditions of acceptance**.*

(ii) The Unexpected: Extra/Additional Work-lists

Unexpected finding or event in a project would normally lead to extra or additional work request.

Any extra/additional work request was challenged and approved in the same manner as the Late Work-lists. However, for fast track project, the committee to review the extra/ additional work would comprise of the personnel who were readily available for the review as and when required.

Variation Order (if applicable) will be prepared by contractor, attaching the completed Project Extra/Additional Work-lists Request Form for endorsement of the Project Manager and approval of the Approving Authority.

The relevant _members of the Technical Team_ will be consulted to resolve the extra/additional work request. As quick decision was essential during the project, the Technical Team Meeting would convene without delay.

*Note : Here we can see **asking the specialist** was applied.*

The project critical path will be reviewed. Should the project duration be extended due to the extra/additional work, Recovery Plan would be enforced such as;
- changing work pattern (overtime, 24 hour work);
- increase manpower, tools or equipment;
- implementing approved nonstandard repair.

Work Patterns

Working hours would be developed after review of the critical path duration and business needs. Normally a 10 hour working day, 7 days a week, would be planned for majority of the work, Monday to Sunday including Public Holiday(s) for fast track project.

However, critical path work would be carried out on a 24 hour continuous basis.

(iii) Commissioning

After the Initial Hand-over Certificates of the work area have been accepted by Client, area commissioning would commence.
*Note : Here we can see **taking precautions** was applied; making partial delivery for customer's **conditions of acceptance** and thus facilitating commissioning work.*

The Commissioning Manager (normally client representative) would take charge of the work area with the Project Manager as the Technical Advisor.

The Daily Coordination Meeting will be replaced with the Daily Commissioning Meeting.

Standby crew, comprising of contractors' personnel would be

arranged to carry out any rework or additional work in shifts cycle on 24 hr. basis until stable commissioning took place.

If any rework is required, and the contractor responsible was identified, the rework would be done by the standby personnel from that contractor. If the contractor's personnel are not available/adequate, the rework would be done by;
- additional personnel from the responsible contractor with no additional cost to company;

or

- any available standby personnel from other contractors, the cost to be charged to the responsible contractor.

If there was any new work on "untouched" area, the work would be done by any available standby personnel, irrespective of whichever contractor .

4.0 Post Project Execution Activities

Post Project Execution activities commence after stable commissioning, which include;
(a) Demobilization;
(b) Final Site Inspection;
(c) *Post Mortem Debrief*;
(d) Project Report.
*Note : Here we can see **taking certain precautions** was applied; lessons learnt from the project work was communicated to relevant parties.*

(a) Demobilization

Demobilization refers to removal of the following from the site:
- all manpower (in-house or contractor);

- all tools/equipment;
- all surplus material;
- all site offices, stores;
- all site office equipment (computer , photocopiers, etc.);
- all temporary work station;
- all redundant equipment, debris, rubbish, dirt, spillage and effluent.

(b) Final Site Inspection

After completion of demobilization, the Project Manager would arrange a site inspection with the Commissioning Manager to ensure that;
- all agreed work has been completed;
- all traces of the project has been removed;
- the work area is clean and tidy;
- no damage has been caused to the work area.

The Project Manager would note any outstanding work, arrange for rework and re-inspection if required.

If the Commissioning Manager was satisfied, he would sign for acceptance of the Final Hand-over Certificate after expiry of the warranty/guarantee period.

(c) Post Mortem Debrief

The Project Manager would arrange for the Post Mortem Debrief, with the participation of the key personnel of the Project Team to cover the following topics:

Topics	Speaker
- Actual vs. Planned w.r.t. to performance in SHE, Quality, Schedule, Duration and Cost	Project Manager
- Original Scope vs. Late, Extra/Additional Work	Planner
- Highlights, Lessons Learnt and Recommendation	Safety Officer Quality Officer Scheduler Cost Control Officer Area Coordinators
- Closing comments	Project Manager M anagement rep.

(d) Project Report

The Project Report would normally be prepared two (2) weeks after the project.

Typical contents of the Project Report are;
- Summary;
- Scope of Work;
- SHE;
- Quality;
- Schedule & Duration;
- Cost;
- Planning & Preparation highlights;
- Project Execution highlights;
- Lessons Learnt & Recommendation.

5.0 Project Communication Plan

The Project Communication Plan would comprise of communication to relevant external/internal parties through meeting, reports, newsletters, briefing, etc. to ensure that all interested parties were _kept well informed at such time that any required corrective or preventive action can be executed timely_.

*Note : Here we can see **taking precautions** was applied; making partial delivery by reporting the work progress for customer's **conditions of acceptance**.*

Chapter 4 : The Principle

Integrating the formulas explained in Chapter 2 will form the problem solving principle. Before you look at the integrated formulas, the writer wish to recap some of the questions or the things to be considered for each formula.

Prepare the Next Definite Step
- Preparing or doing part of the future step which will be rewarded/ recognized and which do not require the preceding step(s) to be done in order to know what is actually required to be done in the preceding step(s);
- Going to the work site to see the opportunities apart from the constraints/obstacles;
- Asking for clarifications that will make the work easier; asking the cause of the problem and alternative solutions, asking the risk/**criticality** of doing nothing, asking where is it critical, asking what had been done to solve the problem, the lessons learnt and the recommendations, asking who can help you, what tools to be used and asking for more details.

Take the Opportunity
- Doing the work without additional cost with the resources assigned to other work at same/nearby area;
- Taking the opportunity to get partial payment after making partial delivery;
- Selling the problem;
  - ✓ To offer the problem to those who need the problem;
  - ✓ To advertise something while solving the problem.

- To reuse the problem against the origin of the problem.

What We Have/Can
- What had been done to solve the problem?
- What do we have and what can we do to solve the problem?
  - ✓ Are there any prepared/local/owned resources-special tool?
  - ✓ Can we do swapping?
  - ✓ Is there any simple way to do it?
  - ✓ Can we use only one than rather multiple?
  - ✓ Can we fix the schedule than rather on as-and-when required basis?
- What had been done <u>elsewhere</u> to solve similar problem? Do we have or can we do that?

Selected Part
First or later (depending on the availability of resources and opportunity), starting from critical or non-critical/changeable part (depending on your confidence) at the applicable part.

Taking Certain Precautions
For potential quality problem
- Modifying or increasing/decreasing what we have/can to *contain, keep away, shield, hide, camouflage, sacrifice, create, swap, use other alternative, re-rate* the potential problem;
- Using **special tool** for difficult work process;
- Audit/check on its compliance to what was planned.
For potential time problem
- Negotiate (see **asking specialist**) with supplier;
- **Learn and teach others to do** the work;
- Using **special tool** for low productivity work process.
For potential cost problem
- Negotiate (see **asking specialist**) with supplier;

- **Learn and teach others to do** the work;
- Use **original suppliers.**

For potential time/quality/cost problem

- Supply to your supplier with your **special tool** to improve the delivery period or work quality but charge your supplier the rental rate;
- Seeking lessons learnt and recommendations from past practitioners;
- Create a system to warn you of the upcoming failure, make what you do changeable and accessible promptly in case of anything go wrong;
- Making **partial delivery** to your customer for his **conditions of acceptance** and partial payment;
- Do nothing where the risk of doing nothing is negligible or doing something can cause more harm than good.

Find the Root Cause

- What are the possible causes? Can we confirm the possible causes quickly? If yes, proceed to confirm, if no, then ask the following questions;
- Where could the problem be, but is not happening? What is the difference in that area from the problem area? Is any of the possible causes unique to the problem area?
- When was the first time the same problem was observed? What is the changes just before the first time the same problem was observed? Can any of the possible causes be related to that changes? Is the timing of the failure predictable (is it age-related)? Is there any symptom before it fail?
- What is the arrangement to prevent the problem? Is any of the possible causes deviating from that arrangement?

Note: The common answer (possible cause) is the most likely cause.

If the above questions could not lead you to the cause of the problem, then you may ask;

- What was the possible causes that was ruled out? Is the assumption still valid?
- Is the problem genuine? Is the measurement right?
- Are the information given correct?

Note: Confirm the most likely cause by testing/simulation.

What is the work that caused the cause of the problem (root cause)? Can the work be substituted by other ongoing work? Can we discontinue the work?

Remaining Part of the Problem
- Other difficult-to-do part of the problem;
- Other potential area that can be affected by similar problem;
- Back-up/contingency plan;
- Action to be taken before the same problem recur at the same area.

What We Want Ultimately
Subject to the customer's correction/confirmation;
- It meet the customer requirement but yet;
- So flexible that it can solve the customer's other problems such that;
- It boost the customer's profit or the product is having low life cycle cost;
- Make the customer feel very safe and secured and;
- Boost the customer reputation or the product/service is recognized worldwide as the best product/service.

Ask the Specialist
Do the work for you free of charge:
- You will increase the supplier's business volume by recommending the product/service to other clients;
- To prove that it will work for the supplier to market its product to other clients;
- Cost/reward sharing with supplier.

Inquire;
- Track record showing clearly the scope of work, client, value and date;
- Application and benefit compared to their competitor (life cycle cost, inter-changeability of parts to existing product, warranty/guarantee, etc.);
- Concerns and how it is being addressed;
- Work process to prepare, operate and maintain the product and the associated rate, productivity, quality test method, SHE precautions;
- List of sub-suppliers (original suppliers) and special tools/equipment;
- Other alternative products;
- Suppliers contact tel., fax., e-mail, address.

Negotiate;
- From the proposed work process to prepare the product/service and the associated rate and productivity, take out from the supplier those work process where it can be done cheaper/faster by owned/other cheaper supplier;
- Performance bond in term of retention money or bank guarantee to assure that the supplier will not quit before completing the work, to make good the product if found defective during the warranty period and as a start up capital (in case of retention money) for you to manage the work;
- Target to complete the work earlier and apply LAD (Liquidated Ascertain Damage). LAD is a kind of penalty that the supplier has to pay if the work delay, normally in the form of deduction from the contract price;
- Do additional work without additional cost.

You may negotiate such that there will be zero out-of-pocket money for you by the following:
- You will pay the supplier after receiving the payment from your customer or after receiving the loans/claims by asking

favorable credit terms from your supplier or pay your supplier after expiry of the warranty/guarantee period;
- Payment by giving your product/service to your supplier;
- Cost/reward sharing;
- Middling.

Certain part, Do it by Ourselves where;
- Life cycle cost of the special tool and other associated resources is lower than asking the specialist to do the work;
- Mobilization time of the specialist is not acceptable for such critical service;
- Asking others to do the work will expose them to your confidential/ secret matters;
- It will add value to your skill and knowledge.

Learn by;
- Comparing with the things you know very well;
- Remember by the initial letter;
- Reciting;
- Doing;
- Teaching others.

Teach others by chain reaction.

Problem Solving Principle

The formulas of the getting the work done faster, better and cheaper may now be integrated to form a problem solving principle as follows:

> **Prepare the next definite step immediately and take the opportunity to solve the problem temporarily using what we have/can at selected part but taking certain precautions.**
>
> **Find out and discontinue the work that caused the problem where the work can be substituted by other ongoing work .**
>
> **For the remaining part of the problem, prepare what we want ultimately by asking the specialist to work together and at certain part, do it by ourselves, learn, teach others and acquire the resources to do the wholesome specialist work in the future.**

Well, that seems too simple to be a good problem solving principle. Now consider the following. The **next definite step, what we have/can, selected part and taking certain precautions** will enable you to be close to achieve zero time. By doing the **next definite step immediately**, you are ahead of time (negative time) and by **solving the problem temporarily** (using **what we have/can at selected part but taking certain precautions**), you will take a little time (positive time). If both are done, then you are deemed to achieve zero time (negative time plus positive time). Taking action on the **remaining part of the problem** will lead you to take action before similar problem recur, therefore you may achieve negative time for future similar problem.

Find out and discontinue the work will enable you to be close to achieve zero mistake. Coupled with getting **what we want ultimately**, you may solve the problem once and for all, therefore you may achieve negative mistake.

Take the opportunity, solve the problem temporarily and **asking the specialist** will enable you to be close to achieve zero cost. By **taking the opportunity**, you may make money while solving the problem (negative cost) and by **solving the problem temporarily** and **asking the specialist**, you may take a little cost (positive cost). If these are done, then the result is zero cost (negative cost plus positive cost) . But if you are creative in **taking the opportunity**, you may even achieve negative cost. **Find out and discontinue the work** may also enable you to achieve negative cost because you save cost by discontinuing the work.

Learn, teach others and acquire the resources to do the wholesome specialist work may enable you to be even closer to achieve the three zeros in the future. It is about enhancing our capability to prepare **what we want ultimately** ourselves before the problem recur.

While getting **what we want ultimately** for a problem, you may **take the opportunity** to prepare the **next definite step** of another problem, therefore making this problem solving principle a cycle by itself. When you solve a problem in this cyclic manner, you are also solving other problems and therefore you may virtually achieve;

- Negative time as you move from **next definite step** to another **next definite step**;
- Negative mistake as you solve a problem once and for all i.e. solving other problems while solving a problem;
- Negative cost as you **take the opportunity** of solving a problem to solve another problem.

The above negatives are the assurance for you to be close enough to achieve zero time, zero mistake and zero cost.

But above all, you need a strong desire to achieve the three negatives in order to settle at the three zeros as in the real world there are a lot of things that can obstruct your way. You also need the confidence that this problem solving principle will work sooner or later.

Looking at Different Perspectives

The above problem solving principle can also be seen in the following perspective:

Theme 1: Selected Part
Prepare the next definite step immediately and take the opportunity to solve the problem temporarily using what we have/can at **selected part** but taking certain precautions.

Theme 2: Discontinue the work
Find the root cause and **discontinue the work** that caused the problem where the work can be substituted by other ongoing work.

Theme 3: Ask the specialist
For the remaining part of the problem, prepare what we want ultimately by **asking the specialist** to work together and at certain part, do it by ourselves, learn, teach others and acquire the resources to do the wholesome specialist work in the future.

The above three themes enable us to solve the problem easily and in a practical manner. Theme 1 ask us to focus at certain thing than rather to solve the whole problem at a time. Theme 2 ask us to solve the problem by doing nothing (discontinuing certain work) than rather doing something. Theme 3 ask us to seek for help (ask the specialist) than rather doing the difficult work all by ourselves.

The above problem solving principle can also be seen in the following perspective:

Prepare the next definite step immediately and take the opportunity to solve the problem temporarily using what we have/can at selected part but taking certain precautions.

Prepare the next definite step (**i.e. find the root cause)** and take the opportunity to solve the problem temporarily using what we have/can (**i.e. discontinue the work that caused the problem)** at selected part (**i.e. where the work can be substituted by other ongoing work)** but taking certain precautions.

Prepare the next definite step (**i.e. for the remaining part of the problem, prepare what we want ultimately)** and take the opportunity to solve the problem temporarily using what we have/can (**i.e. by asking the specialist to work together)** at selected part but taking certain precautions (**i.e. at certain part, do it by ourselves, learn, teach others and acquire the resources to do the wholesome specialist work in the future).**

If the writer remove the words in the brackets, the above problem solving principle may be further simplified as follows:

> Prepare the next definite step immediately and take the opportunity to solve the problem temporarily using what we have/can at selected part but taking certain precautions.

You may wonder why **solve the problem temporarily** and then pull stop. Why there is no permanent solution mentioned? It is because today's permanent solution is tomorrow's temporary solution. An airplane driven by a propeller, once thought to be a permanent solution to fly was replaced by a jet engine. A jet engine was then replaced by a compressed gas for spacecraft. Compressed gas system will eventually be replaced by something new in the future. In short, nothing is permanent in this world except God.

Sometime its quite difficult to think of the **next definite step** especially when the problem is new to you and/or you do not have the opportunity or resources to prepare the **next definite step.** So you may start with something easy-to-do and once you get the momentum, you may be able to do the hard-to-do but effective things. Therefore, for practical reason, you may modify the above problem solving principle as follows:

> Use/do what we have/can immediately at selected part but take the opportunity to prepare the next definite step and take certain precautions.

The above problem solving principle may also be integrated with the way you used to think. The writer hereby introduce the concept **do anything** which means do what you used to do, do what you want to do, do what your boss want you to do, do with what you have/can, do what the majority want, do what you think right, do what you think good or do anything as long that you are not breaking any rule/law though you may be "bending" it. Therefore the above problem solving principle may be seen as follows:

> **Do anything immediately at selected part but take the opportunity to prepare the next definite step and take certain precautions.**

You may think it's ridiculous letting people to do anything. But hold on. It says **do anything at selected part.** Consider the following. Drug is bad for health but at selected part (at certain quantity and with doctor's prescription) it become a medicine. Snakes may be dangerous to you but it also scare away the rats from eating your crops at selected part (at your farm). Kill your enemy may not be your style as you are not a killer/murderer but you may be able to accept this; kill your enemy at selected part (kill the movement of your enemy by stopping the supplies to your enemy). So do anything that you think right but apply it at **selected part.**

CHAPTER 5 : APPLICATION

Application of this problem solving principle may be done in the following ways:

Application No. 1

Level 1
Prepare the next definite step immediately and take the opportunity to solve the problem temporarily by using what we have/can at selected part but taking certain precautions(or do what we have/can or do anything immediately at selected part to solve the problem temporarily and take the opportunity to prepare the next definite step and take certain precautions).

Case 1 : You don't know what is the next definite step, how to take opportunity, what we have/can, selected part and precautions to be taken
Find out the next definite step, how to take opportunity, what we have/can, selected part and precautions to be taken and repeat Level 1 with practicable alternative.

Case 2: Level 1 is not good enough or the problem is critical
Do Level 1 and go to Level 2.

Case 3: Level 1 is good enough
Do Level 1 and stop here.

Level 2
Find out and discontinue the work that caused the problem where the work can be substituted by other ongoing work.

Case 1 : You don't know what is the root cause
Find out the root cause and repeat Level 2 with practicable alternative.

Case 2: Level 2 is not good enough
Do Level 2 and go to Level 3.

Case 3: Level 2 is good enough
Do Level 2 and stop here.

Level 3
For the remaining part of the problem, prepare what we want ultimately by asking the specialist to work together and at certain part, do it by ourselves, learn, teach others and acquire the resources to do the wholesome specialist work in the future.

Case 1 : You don't know what is the remaining part of the problem, what we want ultimately, who are the specialists and certain part
Find out the remaining part of the problem, what we want ultimately, the specialists, certain part and repeat Level 3 with practicable alternative.

Case 2: Level 3 is not good enough or the problem is critical
Do Level 3 and go to Continuity Level.

Case 3: Level 3 is good enough
Do Level 3 and stop here.

Continuity Level

You take the opportunity of preparing what you want ultimately to prepare the next definite step of another problem. Therefore, you will be repeating the same cycle, but solving another problem to solve your current problem. In this way, Continuity Level will assure you with endless ways of solving your problem as there is no ending if you go into a cycle. You will stop only when the overall solution is good enough for you to solve the problem.

Level 1 may be considered the way you approach the problem. Selected part of Level 1, Level 2 to Continuity Level are your justifications or defenses to your Level 1, therefore you have endless justifications/defenses to your decision. You may also use them to defend or justify your past decision or somebody's decision.

Level 1 may be considered the short term solution while Level 2 to Continuity Level may be considered the long term solution.

You may proceed with Level 1 i.e. to prepare the next definite step by doing part of the future major step first without asking questions such as what had been done to solve the problem, the cause and criticality of the problem. It is because;

- You won't lose anything by doing part of the definite future major step regardless of whether the current problem is critical or not or whether you had considered what had been done and the cause of the problem;

- If you start to think first about the cause of the problem, criticality of the problem or what had been done to solve the problem, then you may not be able to apply it to your non-core day-to-day activity. Imagine if your wife ask you to take a towel for her, and you start to ask her why she want the towel, the criticality of taking the towel or what had been done to take the towel, then life will be so slow and boring with that sort of questions. But instead you do part of the future step immediately; you go to the bedroom to change your clothing in preparation for your dinner and you take the opportunity to take your wife's towel. If you cannot find the towel, then you ask why she need the towel so that you can find other alternative to the towel.

You might ask why for all Case 3, you may stop and discontinue application of the remaining principle. It is because you simply cannot afford to apply the whole problem solving principle for everything you do. You need to have priorities in your life. So you apply this problem solving principle to the level where it commensurate with the criticality of the problem. This is the purpose of asking, " Is this solution good enough"?

Application No. 2

Application No. 2 is about solving the problem by asking a series of ten questions:

1)   What is the risk of doing nothing? **Do nothing at negligible part.**
2)   Where and when is it critical?
3)   What are the options (next process, what had been done, what we have/can, go to work site), which option can be done first and what are the precautions to be taken?
Prepare the next definite step immediately and take the opportunity to solve the problem temporarily by using what we have/can at selected part but taking certain precautions .
4)   What are the possible causes? Can we confirm the possible causes quickly? If yes, proceed to confirm, if no, then ask the following questions;

5)   Where could the problem be, but is not happening? What is the difference in that area from the problem area? Is any of the possible causes unique to the problem area?

6)   When was the first time the same problem was observed? What is the changes just before the first time the same problem was observed? Can any of the possible causes be related to that changes? Is the failure predictable; is it age-related, is there any symptom before it fail?

7)   What is the arrangement to prevent the problem. Is any of the possible causes deviate from that arrangement?

8)   What is the most likely cause? If not clear, then;

For critical failure which is predictable, you may arrange to take proactive action at an opportunity just before the predicted failure. For critical failure which is not predictable, you may put a standby unit/solution. If most likely cause is clear, then proceed to next question;

9)   What is the work that cause the most likely cause? Can we discontinue the work? Can the work be substituted by other ongoing work? If yes, then;

Discontinue the work that caused the problem where the work can be substituted by other ongoing work. If no, proceed to next question;

10)   What do we want to do ultimately? Who can help us? Who else?

For the remaining part of the problem, prepare what we want ultimately by asking the specialist to work together and at certain part, do it by ourselves, learn, teach others and acquire the resources to do the wholesome specialist work in the future.

Application No. 3

Application No. 3 is about enabling an idea of a solution, from your thinking or group discussion or your boss idea or someone's idea, regardless of whether it's good or not, to be considered but you add value to the idea instead of killing the idea by the following five checklists:

✓ **Selected part** : Where or when will this idea be suitably applied?

✓ **Next definite step** : What's next? Can we take the opportunity to prepare the next definite step and then modify the idea accordingly?

✓ **Taking certain precautions** : Are there any concerns to implement the idea? What are the precautions to be taken?

✓ **Root cause** : What is the work that caused the problem? Can this work be substituted by other ongoing work? Can we discontinue this work?

✓ **What we want ultimately** : For the remaining part of the problem, can we prepare what we want ultimately by asking the specialist to work together and at certain part, do it by ourselves, learn, teach others and acquire the resources to do the wholesome specialist work in the future?

In fact there are many other ways you can apply the problem solving principle. You can modify the above three applications or you make a completely new application based on the said problem solving principle. It depends on whichever way that suit you.

Examples

Below are some examples on how you can apply this problem solving principle to solve some simple to complicated problems using Application No. 1. It does not mean that this is the only way you can solve the problem when you apply this problem solving principle. Theoretically, by applying this problem solving principle, you have endless ways to solve the problem. You choose the one way that is practicable to be done based on what you have/can, you apply this principle level by level and you stop once you have considered the level is good enough to solve your problem.

While you look at the examples, you may also imagine solving the problem yourself based on what you have learned and whichever practicable way.

Example 1 : Problem : Tall grass at your house compound

Level 1: Prepare the next definite step immediately and take the opportunity to solve the problem temporarily using what we have/can at selected part but taking certain precautions.

You <u>prepare the next definite step</u> by going to the site of the tall grass immediately and warm up to prepare for your routine jogging. Then you <u>take the opportunity</u> to cut the grass with <u>what you have/can</u> (the available grass cutter) before you go for the jogging.

You will start at <u>selected part</u> (the front part of your house where the tall grass is too long and obvious to the public). You <u>take certain precaution</u> by teaching your children to complete the remaining part. You will also <u>take certain precaution</u> by pulling the roots while you cut the grass to stop it from growing again.

Level 2: Find out and discontinue the work that caused the problem where the work can be substituted by other ongoing work.

- What are the possible causes? *Roots not pulled, <u>grass not poisoned,</u> fast growing species of grass.* Can we confirm the possible causes quickly? *No.*

- Where could the problem be, but is not happening? *My neighbor's house compound.* What is the difference in that area from the problem area? *The grass is of the same species but my neighbor used to apply weed killer to poison the grass.* Is any of the possible causes unique to the problem area? *Yes, grass not poisoned.*
- When was the first time the same problem was observed? *Ever since you moved in to the house.* What is the changes just before the first time the same problem was observed? *Don't know.* Can any of the possible causes be related to that changes? *Don't know.* Is the timing of the failure predictable (is it age-related)? *Yes, about one month after cutting.* Is there any symptom before it fail? *Yes, you can see the grass growing.*
- What is the arrangement to prevent the problem. *You ask around and you find out that people normally poison the grass.* Is any of the possible causes deviating from that arrangement? *Yes, grass is not poisoned.*

The common answers to the questions above is that the grass are not poisoned. You may then confirm the cause by poisoning the grass and monitor for any recurrence of the problem. Then you find out the work that caused the problem (the work that you used to do that caused the grass not poisoned is that you are too busy with your routine jogging work). Then you discontinue the jogging work temporarily and substitute it with another form of exercise i.e. the grass poisoning work.

Level 3: For the remaining part of the problem, prepare what we want ultimately by asking the specialist to work together and at certain part, do it by ourselves, learn, teach others and acquire the resources to do the wholesome specialist work in the future.

For remaining part of the problem i.e. before the grass grow again, you may prepare what you want ultimately i.e. landscaping work at your house compound, install security gate, grow some orchids and you may ask a specialist to do it for you. You will inquire few specialists and negotiate with them to get a good deal. You will ask them to start the landscaping work at the front part of your house. When you got to know how the specialist do his work, you will at certain part, do it by yourself i.e. take out certain work scope of the specialist where it can be done cheaper by yourself.

While doing this work yourself, you will learn how the remaining landscaping work is done. You will later employ a cheap labor and teach them to do the remaining landscaping work at the back part of your house. You will pay this cheap labor and the specialist by using the money that you got from selling the orchids that were grown by the specialist.

Continuity Level: You take the opportunity of preparing what you want ultimately to prepare the next definite step of another problem.

While you do the landscaping, gate installation and orchid growing work (what you want ultimately), you will take the opportunity to prepare the next definite step of another problem (discuss with the specialist on how you should renovate your house and also to solve the problem of the corroding gutter........). And you go on with the same cycle for solving the problem of the corroding gutter until you feel the overall solution is good enough to solve the problem of your tall grass.

In the above problem, you may be close enough to achieve;
- Zero time i.e. negative time (because you are implementing your future plan; landscaping, gate installation, orchid

growing and house renovation work) plus little time (to solve the problem temporarily by cutting the grass yourself with available cutter at the front part of your house);

- Zero mistake because you prevent the grass from growing again by just discontinuing your jogging work to have your time to poison the grass;
- Zero cost because you use the sale from the orchids to pay the specialist and the cheap labor.

Example 2 : Problem : How to study at school /university

Level 1: Prepare the next definite step immediately and take the opportunity to solve the problem temporarily using what we have/can at selected part but taking certain precautions .

A conventional manner of studying is that you will go for the class and then you will do the homework/study later in the night or just before exam.

With this problem solving principle, before attending a class tomorrow, you may <u>prepare the next definite step</u> by studying tonight what's going to be taught tomorrow. By doing so, apart being ahead in the knowledge of the subject, you will be able to follow your lecturer throughout the class and being able to ask meaningful question. In this way, you are actually already doing the revision rather than doing the study.

You may also study what's going to be taught in the next semester during the semester break.

With this prior knowledge, you will <u>take the opportunity</u> to focus during the class on the part that you don't understand <u>(use what we have/can at selected part)</u> after your study last night . You <u>take certain precaution</u> by asking your lecturer what's going to be taught tomorrow/next week so that you don't unnecessarily study something else that night.

Level 2: Find out and discontinue the work that caused the problem where the work can be substituted by other ongoing work.

Finding the root cause of wanting to know how to study is not relevant as you want to live a successful life .

Level 3 : For the remaining part of the problem, prepare what we want ultimately by asking the specialist to work together and at certain part, do it by ourselves, learn, teach others and acquire the resources to do the wholesome specialist work in the future.

At remaining part of the problem (remaining part of the subject where it is difficult for you to understand despite your prior study and the given lecture), you want to have a full understanding of the subject such that you can pass your subject with flying colors and apply it in your day-to-day work (what you want ultimately). So you ask the specialist (your top-scorer classmate) to re-explain to you the subject that you don't understand. You may do this on share basis, i.e. you will also tell your specialist what you understand and therefore information sharing take place.

You ask your top scorer classmate the method of studying/remembering and learn so that you can apply it in your future class and teach others to do the same.

Continuity Level: Take the opportunity of preparing what you want ultimately to prepare the next definite step of another problem.

While you discuss with your top-scorer classmate to get full understanding of the subject (<u>preparing what you want ultimately</u>), you may want to <u>take the opportunity</u> to know your classmate better (<u>prepare the next definite step of another problem</u>).

In the above problem, you may be close enough to achieve;
- Zero time i.e. negative time (because you are ahead of time by knowing the subject before you go to the class) plus little time (as you are only focussing in the class on the part that you don't understand after your study in previous night);
- Zero mistake because you discuss with your top scorer classmate on the part that is not clear to you;
- Zero cost because you do not use external specialist/tutor to re-explain to you the subject.

<u>**Example 3 : Problem: How to start a house construction business**</u>

<u>**Level 1: Prepare for the next definite step immediately and take the opportunity to solve the problem temporarily using what we have/can at selected part but taking certain precautions**</u>.

A normal way to start a house construction business would be to;
Step A : Acquire the land;
Step B : Select a contractor;
Step C : Construction work;
Step D : Find the customer;
Step E : Get the reward.

You immediately <u>prepare the next definite step</u> by preparing Step D to find the customer. You ask your potential customers what sort of house they want and why they want it like that in order to find the alternatives. You go to the site and assess the constraints and opportunities. You take the opportunity of having found potential customers and assessed the work site to proceed with Step B i.e. to tender out the design and construction work to reliable contractors (do what we have/can at selected part) and assure the tenderer of payment guarantee with the projected demand from potential customers. By competitive bidding, you select the technically acceptable and lowest tenderer for negotiation. Then you may impose the retention money as one of the terms and conditions for award of the contract. You start the negotiation and later settle at 10% retention money.

With the retention money, you take the opportunity to go to Step A; acquire the land by negotiating with the land owner (do what we have/can at selected part):

- Pay him fully for the land if the retention money is adequate or;
- Pay him down payment; the remaining payment to be made after completion of the project or;
- Get him to allow you to work on his land and become shareholder.

With the agreement signed between you and the contractor, you take the opportunity to ask for loans from selected banks (do what we have/can at selected part) and you use that money to pay the contractor progressively in order to motivate the contractor or release its burden in the initial phase of the project.

You stress to the contractor to complete Phase 1 of the project (do what we have/can at selected part), so that you can start to deliver the house to your customer while completing the other phases of the project. You are now again ahead of time in Step

E by getting the reward and you use the reward to make progressive payment to the contractor.

You anticipate delay in the project, so you <u>take certain precautions</u>;
- Impose LAD;
- You split the work area among 2 contractors, so that they will compete with each other to complete the work and as a back up to each other if one contractor could not perform.

You anticipate quality problem, so you <u>take certain precautions</u>;
- Invite potential customers to review the design and audit the construction work to ensure zero mistake;
- Specify in the contract of your right to takeaway the contractor's scope of work in parts or in whole if they don't perform and you replace them with the other contractor.

<u>Level 2: Find out and discontinue the work that caused the problem where the work can be substituted by other ongoing work.</u>

Finding the root cause of wanting to start a house construction business is not relevant as you want to make money out of it.

<u>Level 3: For the remaining part of the problem, prepare what we want ultimately by asking the specialist to work together and at certain part, do it by ourselves, learn, teach others and acquire the resources to do the wholesome work in the future .</u>

For Phase 2 (<u>remaining part of the problem</u>), the difficult part of the project, you prepare <u>what you want ultimately</u> (build luxurious and secured house using low life cycle cost material). You select <u>specialist</u> contractor in the same manner as above. You ask either one of the Phase 1 contractors to <u>do certain part by themselves</u> i.e. some of the work process of the specialist contractor which is expensive but can be done by the Phase 1 contractor.

Then you ask the Phase 1 contractor to <u>learn</u> from the specialist contractor to do the wholesome specialist work while working together with the specialist contractor. Then the Phase 1 contractor will be assigned to complete Phase 3 of the project (also quite difficult part) with Phase 1 contractor's cheaper rate without engaging the expensive specialist contractor.

<u>**Continuity Level: You take the opportunity of preparing what you want ultimately to prepare the next definite step of another problem.**</u>

You may also want the specialist contractor to include some exclusive furniture free of charge (<u>prepare the next definite step of another problem</u>) in the difficult-to-do but better house (<u>what you want ultimately</u>).

In the above problem, you may be close enough to achieve;
- Zero time i.e. negative time (because you are ahead of time by getting the reward from retention money, loans and sale of the Phase 1 house) plus little time (to prepare the agreement and complete Phase 1 house);
- Zero mistake because you ask the potential customers to review the design and check the construction work and you use specialist contractor to built the luxurious, secured and low life cycle cost Phase 2 house;
- Zero cost because you use the retention money, bank loans and the money from sale of Phase 1 house to pay the contractor progressively.

Example 4 : Problem: A tiger attacking the cattle in a village

Level 1: Prepare the next definite step immediately and take the opportunity to solve the problem temporarily using what we have/can at selected part but taking certain precautions .

You don't know what to do, so you ask the villagers why the tiger would attack the cattle, the criticality of the problem and what had been done to address this problem. You find out that:

- Nobody know why the tiger attack except for possibility of no food in the jungle;
- The consequence of doing nothing is more cattle will die and the probability based on the history, is that the cattle will die in the next 2-3 days;
- Nothing had been done to address the problem. Nobody dare to go into the jungle anymore.

You <u>prepare the next definite step</u> by going to the zoo and discuss with the officials of the action to be taken when you had caught the tiger. From the discussion, you noted how the tiger was caught in other villages and you realize that the media, National Geographic, Discovery are very interested to film the tiger's catching while the tiger hunters from the zoo are very interested to catch the tiger.

You <u>will take the opportunity</u> by asking the media, National Geographic, Discovery and tiger hunters to sponsor the activity of catching the tiger.

With little knowledge of catching the tiger, the best thing most villagers can do is to stay away from the jungle, especially at the site of attack (do <u>what we have/can at selected part</u>)

You ask the villagers, especially the village head and those who depend on the jungle for their food <u>to take certain precaution</u>

i.e. stay away from the jungle and in turn, they teach other villagers to do the same.

You also take certain precaution by asking the villagers to set a patrol in large group on rotation basis to monitor and prevent people from entering the jungle. You ask the villagers their conditions of acceptance on your plan and the remaining plan listed below.

Level 2: Find out and discontinue the work that caused the problem where the work can be substituted by other ongoing work.

- What are the possible causes? *No food in the jungle, cattle reared nearby the jungle, tiger wanted to take revenge.* Can we confirm the possible causes quickly? *No.*
- Where could the problem be, but is not happening? *Nearby village.* What is the difference in that area from the problem area? Is any of the possible causes unique to the problem area? *In this village, the cattle is reared nearby the jungle.*
- When was the first time the same problem was observed? *1990.* What is the changes just before the first time the same problem was observed? *Before that the people did not rear the cattle nearby the jungle.* Is the timing of the failure predictable? *No.* Is there any symptom before it fail? *No*
- What is the arrangement to prevent the problem. *You ask the specialist and you find out that the food of the tiger should not be seen nearby.* Is any of the possible causes deviating from that arrangement? *Yes, the cattle is reared nearby the jungle.*

The common answer is rearing the cattle nearby the jungle, so this is the most likely cause . Therefore, you ask the villagers to solve the problem by discontinuing the work that caused the problem i.e. discontinue the rearing of the cattle nearby the jungle and find out other suitable place.

Level 3: For the remaining part of the problem, prepare what we want ultimately by asking those specialist to work together and at certain part, do it by ourselves, learn, teach others and acquire the resources to do the wholesome specialist work in the future.

What we want ultimately is to catch the tiger and any other family of the tiger nearby such that there will be absolutely no more attack from any tigers. You also want to know from the tiger hunter what to do when approaching a tiger. You had asked the specialist (tiger hunters from the zoo) to do it free of charge and they had agreed. You had asked the work process to catch the tiger and you find out that at certain part (waiting for the tiger to eat the bait) would be best done with the help of volunteers (do it by ourselves) on shift basis.

You ask few volunteers to participate in the catching, learn and teach others so that eventually they will become local tiger hunters.

Continuity Level: You take the opportunity of preparing what you want ultimately to prepare the next definite step of another problem.

While you catch the tigers (prepare what you want ultimately), you may take the opportunity to prepare the next definite step of another problem i.e. to explore the jungle to see how it can be improved for those who depend on it for food.

In the above problem, you may be close enough to achieve;
* Zero time i.e. negative time (because you had arranged with the zoo on the thing to do when you had caught the

tiger) plus little time (to ask the villagers to stay away from the jungle to solve the problem temporarily);

- Zero mistake because you ask the specialist to catch the tiger and you ask the villagers to discontinue rearing the cattle at the jungle;
- Zero cost because you use the reward from the media, National Geographic and Discovery to sponsor the activity of catching the tiger and the zoo personnel to catch the tiger free of charge.

Example 5 : Problem: You love your girlfriend very much and you think your girlfriend also loves you. You want to marry her but your mother disagree. Your mother tells you that your girlfriend is not good for you. Your mother tells you to choose either her or your girlfriend.

Level 1: Prepare the next definite step immediately and take the opportunity to solve the problem temporarily using what we have/can at selected part but taking certain precautions .

You prepare the next definite step by proceeding for an engagement with your girlfriend and take the opportunity to assess whether your girlfriend really love you by displaying some of your bad habits (do what we have/can at selected part). But you take certain precaution of not doing something during the engagement that leave you with no choice but to marry her. You also tell your mother that this engagement will be a real test for your girlfriend.

Level 2: Find out and discontinue the work that caused the problem where the work can be substituted by other ongoing work.
Problem: Your mother does not like your girlfriend

- What are the possible causes? *Your girlfriend exhibits bad habits, your girlfriend is not beautiful enough, your mother has other preference.* Can we confirm the possible causes quickly? *No, your mother does not want to talk about it.*
- Where could the problem be, but is not happening? *Your brother's wife seems similar in her outlook with your girlfriend.* What is the difference in your girlfriend and your brother's wife? *Your brother's wife has a pleasant way when greeting somebody and display some good manners. Your girlfriend is a quiet girl and seems arrogant (bad habit).* Is any of the possible causes unique to the problem area? *Yes, your girlfriend exhibits bad habits.*
- When was the first time the same problem was observed? *This is the first time.* What is the changes just before the first time the same problem was observed? Is any of the possible causes be related to that changes? *You don't know.* Is the timing of the failure predictable? *No.* Is there any symptom before it fail? *No.*
- What is the arrangement to prevent the problem. *To prevent the dislike from your mother, your girlfriend should exhibit good habit and demonstrate that she loves you.* Is any of the possible causes deviating from that arrangement? *Yes, your girlfriend exhibits bad habits.*

The common answer is that your girlfriend exhibits bad habit, so this is the most likely cause. You ask your girlfriend to discontinue bad habit and substitute with good habit, which is something that your girlfriend have but just that she is shy with your mother.

Level 3: For the remaining part of the problem, prepare what we want ultimately by asking those specialist to work together and at certain part, do it by ourselves, learn, teach others and acquire the resources to do the wholesome specialist work in the future.

For the remaining part of the problem (complete assessment on your girlfriend), you also ask the help of your father (specialist). You learn from your father his method of assessment so that you can teach your children in the future.

Continuity Level: You take the opportunity of preparing what you want ultimately to prepare the next definite step of another problem.

While your father carry out the assessment (what you want ultimately), you prepare the next definite step of another problem by asking your father to explain to your mother of the good things about your girlfriend so that she may change her perception on your girlfriend.

In the above problem, you may be close enough to achieve;
- Zero time i.e. negative time (because you are already engaged with your girlfriend) plus little time (to assess your girlfriend by displaying some of your bad habits);
- Zero mistake because you take the precaution of not committing for a marriage, you ask your girlfriend to display good habits and you ask your father (local specialist) to help you in the assessment;
- Zero cost because you ask your father with no cost to make the assessment.

Example 6 : Problem: A fire break in your refinery. You have to shutdown your plant and fight the fire. Your ship is just half loaded with oil. An important customer need the ship to be fully loaded or else the contract will be terminated. The journalists have swamped into your plant. You are the Human Resource Manager. The Plant Manager is on medical leave.

The Managing Director order you to take charge as you are the most senior person around.

Level 1: Prepare the next definite step immediately and take the opportunity to solve the problem temporarily using what we have/can at selected part but taking certain precautions .

Problem 1: Fire
Solution: You don't know about fire-fighting so you ask what are the steps in fire-fighting. Your in-house firefighters tell you that first they will try to stop the fire and then they will try to cool off the surrounding equipment so as not to catch fire. So you prepare the next definite step by telling them to cool off the surrounding equipment first, then they will take the opportunity to stop the fire with what they have at the source of the fire (use what we have/can at selected part) . The firefighters will take all the precautions to be in a safe position.

Problem 2: Ship only half loaded
Solution: The next step after loading is for the ship to sail to customer's terminal. So you prepare the next definite step by asking the ship to sail immediately to customer's terminal with half loaded for safety reason. Then you find out which terminals are available (including competitor's terminal) along the route to your customer's terminal and take the opportunity to fully load your ship (do what we have/can at selected part). You may take certain precaution by contacting them well in advance to fully load your ship and send a good negotiator if required.

Level 2: Find out and discontinue the work that caused the problem where the work can be substituted by other ongoing work.
* What are the possible causes? *Hot work at non-gas free area, availability of pyrophoric iron (self igniting chemical),*

use of sparking tool. Can we confirm the possible causes quickly? *No.*

- Where could the problem be, but is not happening? *There was also hot work at nearby area, but there was no fire.* What is the difference in nearby area from this area? Is any of the possible causes unique in the problem area? *In this area, the gas freeing activity was done in a rush manner (resulting in <u>non-gas free area</u>) due to oil production requirement.*
- When was the first time the same problem was observed? *This is the first time.* What is the changes just before the first time the same problem was observed? *Before the fire, there was a welding work (<u>hot work</u>) conducted on a pipeline where nitrogen purging (gas freeing) was done in a rush.* Is the timing of the failure predictable? *No.* Is there any symptom before it fail? *No*
- What is the arrangement to prevent the problem. *To prevent the fire, either one or more of the following should not be available; source of ignition (e.g. <u>hot work</u>), fuel and oxygen.* Is any of the possible causes deviating from that arrangement? *Yes, there was <u>hot work</u> and the line was <u>not</u> <u>completely gas free</u> (fuel is available) due to the rush in work.*

The common answer is <u>hot work at non-gas free area</u>, so this is the most likely cause. You cannot discontinue the hot work as you need the pipe to be repaired but you ask the operators to discontinue the work that caused the problem i.e. rush purging work in the future.

<u>**Level 3: For the remaining part of the problem, prepare what we want ultimately by asking those specialist to work together and at certain part, do it by ourselves, learn, teach others and acquire the resources to do the wholesome specialist work in the future.**</u>

Problem 1: Fire

Solution: For <u>remaining part of the problem</u> (remaining fire fighting work), you want the fire to be put off completely (<u>what we want ultimately</u>) by mobilizing the <u>specialist</u> (integrated fire-fighting team made up of the state firefighters and other firefighter from other nearby refineries/industries) to assist your in-house firefighters. The method of fire-fighting by these specialist will be <u>learned</u>, practiced and later to be <u>taught to other</u> in-house firefighters. .

Problem 2: Ship only half loaded

Solution: Before the problem recur (<u>remaining part of the problem</u>), you may engage a <u>specialist</u> negotiator and legal officer to prepare a long term agreement with other oil refineries (<u>what we want ultimately</u>), especially those located at the route to your customer's terminal, for the supply of oil such that one can supply oil to each other during crisis. You may involve your in-house legal officer to participate and <u>learn</u> the tricks of the negotiation and contract preparation work and share the lessons learnt (<u>teach others</u>).

<u>**Continuity Level: You take the opportunity of preparing what you want ultimately to prepare the next definite step of another problem**</u>.

Problem 1: Fire

Solution: While you mobilize the specialist firefighters (<u>what you want ultimately</u>), you may also <u>prepare the next definite step of another problem</u> by asking them to review the existing design, operation and maintenance system with respect to fire prevention. You may then<u> take the opportunity</u> to ask the journalists to take pictures at selected part of the damages for insurance claim after the fire has been put down.

Problem 2: Ship only half loaded

Solution: While you prepare the long term agreement (<u>what you want ultimately</u>), you may want to strike other agreement e.g. sharing of best practices for mutual benefit (<u>prepare the next definite step of another problem</u>.

In the above problem, you may be close enough to achieve;

- Zero time i.e. negative time (because you cool off surrounding equipment and ask the ship to sail immediately) plus little time (to fight the fire with the in-house firefighters and to ask the other oil refinery to fully load your ship);
- Zero mistake because you prevent the fire from recurring by discontinuing rush line purging work and engaged the specialist firefighters;
- Zero cost because you claim the cost to repair the damage from insurance.

Comments on Examples

Some people were doubtful that the given examples will work in the real world. The writer said to them to try it first and if they still think that it wouldn't work or too complicated or seemed not right, then they may, for a start, apply the following simple principle:

Do anything (that they think right) **immediately at selected part but take the opportunity to prepare the next definite step and take certain precautions. Target to achieve negative time, negative mistake and negative cost. Believe that it will work sooner or later.**

Do anything will enable work to start immediately when you are confused or you don't know what to do. **Selected part, next definite step and taking certain precautions** will control the impact of the work to meet your requirements with respect to time, quality and cost. Nevertheless, equally important is the desire or target to achieve the three zeros if not the negatives. With this target, ideas to achieve the three zeros will come sooner or later. Without this target, even a perfect problem solving principle will not work.

There are certain businessmen who have this working principle; doing business is not how much you can earn, but how much you can save; in other words their target is similar to zero cost. This target drives them to do unusual things such as negotiating to pay their suppliers not by money, but by selling their product or services. They will ask for interest free credit terms such that they will pay their suppliers only when they get the payment from their customer. They will save about 80% of their income for investment. They will save even if it means a dollar a day, because a dollar a day means 365 dollar a year and with good investment this 365 dollar can turn into millions. How? Consider a 100% profit margin. First profit will generate 730 dollars. If 730 dollars is reinvested, the second profit will generate 1460 dollars. If 1460 dollars is reinvested, the third profit will generate 2920 dollars and if this continue, the 12th profit will generate 1,495,040 dollars. Suppose that each investment yield the profit in a month, then these businessmen can become a millionaire in a year. Of course, this is an ideal situation and may not be practical in certain area. The message is that we have to target high; zero time, zero mistake, zero cost, then we will do a lot of magic.

There are certain managers who have no schedule in work; they want everything to be done by today if not yesterday, in other words their target is similar to zero time. This target drives them to find a quicker alternative, drives them to test their ideas in the real world immediately than rather spending their time on speculating the weaknesses of their ideas, drives them to modify proven ideas than rather reinvent the wheel to meet the requirements and drives them to be proactive. To certain extent, by doing things faster, you do things better because you will know the real weaknesses of your ideas in a short time and you will have ample time to modify those ideas to meet the requirements before the actual deadline comes.

Of course, for certain things, you will not be close to achieve zero time, zero mistake and zero cost in just one attempt. If not now, you will achieve them sooner or later. Imagine that you are requested to do a completely new thing i.e. to go to Mars at zero time, zero mistake and zero cost. You will not know now what is the temporary solution and next definite step, so you will not achieve zero time. You will not know now the potential problems that you will face as there are so many uncertainties, so you will not achieve zero mistake. The cost will be billions of dollars and nobody will want to share the cost with you or give you the loans as there is no certainty in the payback, so you will not achieve zero cost. But over time, when you (or your great grand children) persistently learn from others' mistakes to do the work with zero mistake and you do it yourself or teach those people who will charge you minimal cost to do the work and you get the sponsors after a convincing implementation plan and certainty of payback and you reach Mars before the request recur, you (or your great grand children) would have fulfilled this request in the future with zero time, zero mistake and zero cost.

The definition of the three zeros in this book may not be the same as what you expect of the three zeros, but this problem solving principle should be a good start for you to eventually achieve your desired zero time, zero mistake and zero cost with integration to your way of thinking and with persistent learning. We just need to start somewhere to achieve something.

CONCLUSION

The writer believes in the following as the nature of problem:

> **Problem can never be eliminated. It can only be changed from one form to another form.**

To solve a problem in view of time, quality and cost, the writer says:

> **Prepare the next definite step immediately and take the opportunity to solve the problem temporarily using what we have/can at selected part but taking certain precautions.**
>
> **Find out and discontinue the work that caused the problem where the work can be substituted by other ongoing work .**
>
> **For the remaining part of the problem, prepare what we want ultimately by asking the specialist to work together and at certain part, do it by ourselves, learn, teach others and acquire the resources to do the wholesome specialist work in the future.**

The above problem solving principle may be further simplified or made more practical as follows:

> **Use/do what we have/can (or do anything) immediately at selected part but take the opportunity to prepare the next definite step and take certain precautions.**

This problem solving principle is made by integrating the chosen formulas to do the work faster, better and cheaper. The result of this integration is close to zero time, zero mistake and zero cost when applied with a strong desire for negative time/mistake/cost and the confidence that this problem solving principle will work sooner or later. We may be even closer to achieve the three zeros in the future when we have a stronger desire to learn, teach others and acquire the resources to do the wholesome specialist work ourselves before the problem recur or before our customer make the order.

Your desired zero time, zero mistake and zero cost may be achievable if you integrate this problem solving principle with your way of thinking.

<u>The writer advises readers not to read only this chapter to get the gist of the book as the meaning of the terms used may not be the same as what the readers might have understood before reading this book.</u>

What's been told in this book is the structure, roof, walls, ceilings and floor of a house. It is only at principle level. You can live in the house now but you need the chair, table, furniture, carpet, etc. to be comfortable. You need specific ideas/alternatives to apply this problem solving principle in the real world. This problem solving principle is also a processor; you need to give the input to get the output. But you must also remember that no matter how good is the processor, if rubbish input, then rubbish output.

However, it doesn't mean that you cannot apply this problem solving principle now because the writer believes you have already some specific ideas/alternatives of the required chair, table, furniture, carpet, etc. For certain cases, you just need to ask a lot to apply this problem solving principle. The next edition may give you a wider choices of chair, table, furniture, carpet, etc. to choose from, whichever is practicable for you, therefore you may be able to think of a solution quickly without too much asking.

So till then, get in touch again.

TERMINOLOGY

The terms arranged in alphabetical order below are based on the writer's perspective and it may differ with what you might understand before reading this book.

Asking the specialist refers to making an inquiry to a number of specialists and conducting negotiation with selected specialist to get a good deal.

Conditions of acceptance are the conditions stipulated by those affected by the decision in order for them to accept the decision.

Criticality is the consequence (the consequence of doing nothing with respect to SHE, economic and reputation) multiply the probability (the probability that the adverse consequence will be likely to happen based on history or logic).

Do anything means do what you used to do, do what you want to do, do what your boss want you to do, do with what you have/can, do what the majority want, do what you think right, do what you think good, do anything as long that you are not breaking any rule/law though you may be "bending" it.

Life cycle cost of a product is the net present value (NPV) of the product after considering the cost of acquisition, cost of sustaining (operation and maintenance) during its useful life and cost of decommissioning (phasing out, disposal).

Negative Time : When you act before the problem occur (or when you deliver the product/service before the customer make the order), you are deemed to do it with negative time.

Negative Mistake : When you solve the problem once and for all (or when you deliver a product/service that exceed your customer's requirement), you are deemed to do it with negative mistake.

Negative Cost : When you make money instead of incurring cost while you solve the problem, you are deemed to do it with negative cost.

Next definite step is a future step which is definite to be done regardless of the preceding step and which will be rewarded or recognized.

Partial delivery means delivering the product/service to the customer in stages/phases.

Remaining part of the problem can be the other difficult-to-do part of the problem, other potential area that can be affected by similar problem, back-up/contingency plan or the action to be taken before the same problem recur.

Root cause is the cause of a problem that if been addressed will prevent recurrence of the problem.

Do at **selected part** means do it first or later (depending on its practicality), starting from critical or non-critical part (depending on your confidence) at the applicable part.

Swapping is about taking out the product being currently used to replace another similar defective product.

Taking certain precaution is about anticipating potential time, quality and cost problem when you want to do something and preparing to mitigate that potential problem.

What we have/can means what we have done, what do we have and what can we do.

What we want ultimately, subject to your customer's correction and confirmation, is the thing that solve your customer's problem once & for all i.e. it meets the customer requirement but yet so flexible that it can solve the customer's other problems such that it boost the customer's profit or the product is having low **life cycle cost,** make the customer feel very safe and secured and boost the customer reputation or the product/service is recognized worldwide as the best product/service.

Zero Time : When a problem occur (or when your customer make an order) and you solve the problem (or deliver the required product/ service) immediately, you are deemed to do it at zero time.

Zero Mistake : When the problem do not recur after you had solved the problem (or when your final product/service is accepted and no subsequent rejection is made), you are deemed to do it with zero mistake.
Note: In this context, you are allowed to make mistake in your initial product in order to make zero mistake in your final product.

Zero Cost : When you solve the problem with no out-of-pocket money, you are deemed to do it with zero cost.

- END -